Good Grief

Good Grief

A True Story of Love, Loss, and New Life

Sue Borrows LaRue
~with Diane Brown

Elm Hill

A Division of
HarperCollins Christian Publishing

www.elmhillbooks.com

Good Grief

A True Story of Love, Loss, and New Life

Published in Nashville, Tennessee, by Elm Hill, an imprint of Thomas Nelson. Elm Hill and Thomas Nelson are registered trademarks of HarperCollins Christian Publishing, Inc.

Elm Hill titles may be purchased in bulk for educational, business, fund-raising, or sales promotional use. For information, please e-mail SpecialMarkets@ThomasNelson.com.

Library of Congress Cataloging-in-Publication Data

Library of Congress Control Number: 2019933270

Pre-Launch ISBN 978-0-310107682

ISBN 978-0-310107644 (Paperback)
ISBN 978-0-310107651 (Hardbound)
ISBN 978-0-310107668 (eBook)

Contents

Foreword

When Suzie and I began working together, I knew very little about her. I had suffered loss, but wasn't prepared for the depth of her anguish. Though I wasn't raised with an understanding of God's personal plan and love for each of us and did not know about the reality of the Holy Spirit and His activity in our world, God was about to reveal Himself to me through her journey.

Her walk of faith is an intimate one. No matter what, Jesus has always been "MY Jesus" to Suzie. Just as King David addressed the Lord God Almighty as "My Lord," Sue says "My Jesus" with all the reverence, adoration, and depth of feeling of one calling out my Dearest, my Beloved, or my friend. Throughout her life, Jesus has been her Shepherd, Savior, and Hope of Glory. To Suzie, He is, and has always been, "Emmanuel, God with Us."

Her story is one of disappointment and grief, of crying out to Him in distress; of asking, hoping, waiting, and trusting. Ultimately hers is a story of transformation. The Bible says, "Eye has not seen, nor ear heard, nor have entered into the heart of man the things which God has prepared for those who love Him." (1 Corinthians 2:9, NKJV) Suzie could not have created or attained for herself the solace and provision that God has freely given to her. I have witnessed His miraculous presence and leading in her life, and my faith has grown exponentially.

The Good News is that God is no respecter of persons. Jesus promises all who call on Him: "Ask, it will be given to you; seek, and you will find; knock and it will be opened to you. For everyone who asks receives, and he who seeks finds, and to him who knocks, it will be opened." (Matthew 7:7–8, NIV) If we receive Him, His Word assures us, "Then you will experience God's peace, which exceeds anything we can understand. His peace will guard your hearts and minds as you live in Christ Jesus." (Philippians 4:7, NLT)

This is what Suzie did. She sought the Lord and He answered her. She received His surpassing peace and so much more. I hope as you read, you dare to believe that the Lord Suzie loves loves you, and that His saving grace, mercy, comfort, and transforming power are available to all. May her story inspire you, as it has inspired me, to seek God. And just as Suzie did, may you come to trust Him to fulfill His unique purpose for your life which will surely exceed all that you could ever ask, imagine, or think.

> "And we know that God causes all things to work together for good to those who love God, to those who are called according to His purpose."
>
> (Romans 8:28, NKJV)

Prologue

Wow! I just can't tell you what this three-year writing venture has meant to me. Looking back at God's incredible presence in the midst of my grief has healed my heart and grown my relationship with God. I hope that whether you have zero faith or "mustard seed"-sized faith, you will walk away with oversized faith. It was only because of the Lord's prompting and gentle nudging that this book has come to be. I have tried to be open and real throughout. I'm a bit spunky by nature. I love to laugh. I love my Jesus more than I can ever express with mere words.

You may find some of the stories hard to believe, but every word is true; the laughter, tears, brokenness, fears, meltdowns, and victory. The purpose of this book is to show you not only how real God is, but also how much He loves you. He gave His life for you and with that kind of investment, you can trust His love for you and His ability to draw out of you what I know He's planted in you just as He has done in me. He is personally interested in all of us, and wants to work in a deeper way in our lives. I invite you to experience the revealing hand and the tangible presence of God throughout this story. Enjoy!

Dedication

This book is dedicated to the Lord Jesus Christ, Daryle Wayne Borrows, and C. Diane LaRue.

To my son Rick: thank you for your strong arm of love and protection and your many hugs. I love you, my son. To my daughter, Stephanie, and my son-in-law, Kevin: there are no words to describe how grateful I am for your unfailing love. Steph, you were my rock. To my granddaughter Madelyn: you will never know the comfort and joy you brought to my hurting heart. You were a little light in the darkness. To my granddaughter Rebekah: you are a precious gift who ushered a new season of God's grace into my life. You both bring such happiness. My love for you is indescribable.

Huge thanks to my parents Randy and Jessie Hart. I could not have gotten through all this without your constant love and support. You did anything I needed without question or complaint. You were there for me in every way, literally. I am forever grateful. I love you both very much.

To my sister Tracey: thank you for relentlessly praying and reaching out to me when it wasn't easy. You were always there for me. I love you. To my niece Taylor: thank you for being a refuge during our girls' nights. You are such a blessing to me. To my nephew Kacey: you were always ready to help me with anything. You never said "No." Thank you. To my brother Paul: thank you for all your loving advice, your care and concern. No one could make me laugh through my tears like you.

To Daryle's family: I love you all.

To my best friend Michelle: I am eternally grateful for you and for being there 24/7 through the storm. To my dear friends, Jan and Dan: I am amazed at how the Lord used you both to bless my life. I thank you and love you. To Veronica, my dear friend: your powerful prayers and words of encouragement enriched my life. To my late friend Debbie R.: she was faithful to deliver a word from the Lord to encourage our hearts I will always be grateful.

To Megan and Ryan: you are a blessing from God. To my granddaughter Jade: you light up my life. To Ben, Elizabeth, Elijah, and Lucie: Thank you for the laughter you bring. I am honored to journey together in this next season of life with you. Thank you for your kindness to me. I love you all.

To my editor Diane Brown: what a beautiful conduit you are. Your ability to hear the Holy Spirit, to capture our thoughts, to preserve our voice, and to guide our story was exceptional! I love you.

Special thanks to Reverend David and Kathy Walker, Reverend Nathan Pimentel and Pastor John Costa. I love you all.

To my "H2" Bruce Wayne LaRue: my heart is yours.

PART I

LIFE WITH MY LOVE

CHAPTER 1

THE "GOOD" LIFE

Life with Daryle was good. Little did we realize that our "good life" was about to take a devastating and grueling turn that began with a simple question....

"Mr. Borrows. Who is the president of the United States?" asked the nurse at St. Luke's Hospital as she stood behind the dull, scratched, Plexiglas partition. My heart pounded rapidly as my eyes met my mom's and we peered into Daryle's face. As I waited for Daryle to answer, I knew we were in trouble. The emergency room clamor faded as we honed in on Daryle counting his fingers. After what felt like an eternity, he finally said, "Obama." The look on his face seemed to indicate he wasn't certain of his answer, but went with it anyway.

"What day is it?" "What month is it?" "Do you know your birthday?" Question after question determined that he needed immediate attention. After the interrogation was over, I asked him, "Honey, why did it take you so long to answer about the president?"

He responded, "I was counting back from President Reagan."

My heart sank! May 7, 2012 quickly became, and is now forever etched in my mind as, the most frightening and longest day of my life. Earlier in the week, Wednesday, May 2, we were at Bible study, and our pastor abruptly stopped speaking in the middle of his lesson, looked up from his notes, and said, "The Lord just told me to share Psalm 46:1–10. It's for someone here." These verses state:

[1]God is our refuge and strength,
an ever-present help in trouble.
[2]Therefore we will not fear, though the earth give way
and the mountains fall into the heart of the sea,
[3]though its waters roar and foam
and the mountains quake with their surging.
[4]There is a river whose streams make glad the city of God,
the holy place where the Most High dwells.
[5]God is within her, she will not fall;
God will help her at break of day.
[6]Nations are in uproar, kingdoms fall;
he lifts his voice, the earth melts.
[7]The Lord Almighty is with us;
the God of Jacob is our fortress.
[8]Come and see what the Lord has done,
the desolations he has brought on the earth.
[9]He makes wars cease
to the ends of the earth.
He breaks the bow and shatters the spear;
he burns the shields with fire.
[10]He says, "Be still, and know that I am God."

– Psalm 46:1–10, NIV

I turned to Daryle and said, "Gee, I hope that's not for us!"

On Friday, May 4th, Daryle came home from work exhausted, complaining that his job was killing him. He was tripping over his own feet, confused and cranky. I said, "Love, jump in the shower. Have some dinner. Let me rub your back. Then just get some sleep. That will help."

Feeling a bit better the next day, Daryle hoped to fulfill his commitment to drive some men to a church convention. Though he didn't really feel well enough to go, he did it anyway. The drive to their destination took an hour and a half. An hour into the convention, he called me and asked, "Can you come get me? I have a terrible headache." My best friend Michelle happened to be at my house, so we hopped in the car and drove to him. He slept all the way home, and then slept into the night. Waking up the next morning, he said he felt a little better, so he began to prepare for our Sunday service at church where he was the worship leader. Once at church he began practicing, but when I arrived a little later and went to check on him, I could not find him anywhere. I received a text from him explaining that he had to go home to change his clothes because he had had an "accident." He expressed his frustration with his body because he just couldn't understand what was happening. Nor could I.

Just a couple of months before, we had taken time off for our wedding anniversary. We went out of town, stayed in a hotel, went out to dinner and to a jazz concert, and lazed in the hotel pool and hot tub. It was all so perfect, too perfect maybe. Everything was amazing. As we gazed into each other's eyes, I suddenly had an overwhelming fear that it was too good to be true and asked Daryle, "Are we going to die?"

He responded, "What in the world? Why would you think that?"

"Honestly, I don't know. Something feels strange."

"Well, honey, I'm not going anywhere. We are together forever."

"Yes, love. You are right!"

After our romantic weekend, Daryle left for work driving his large delivery truck towards Boston. Around 9:00 a.m. he called me and said, "Honey, I'm having trouble concentrating on the road. I keep going into the breakdown lane."

"That's it!" I said. "Pull over somewhere safe. I'm coming to get you to take you to the ER."

As I left my house, I grabbed my parents and drove over an hour to find him. His boss met us at the truck. He was surprised to find my husband so disoriented. I told him I would call later with Daryle's test results. We were all wondering what on earth could cause such odd symptoms. I thought it might be Lyme disease, a concussion, or maybe some swelling on the brain. I pressed my mother, the nurse in the family, as to what it might be. She could only reassure me that they would figure it out.

We arrived at the ER and I watched as my six-foot, light-brown-haired, blue-eyed hubby was "worked on" by the medical staff. I remember thinking, "Wow! What a frenzy!" I was stunned by the number of people, equipment, and procedures. There were needles and multicolored wires everywhere, and they took blood continually. As they prepped him for a CAT scan of his brain, I could only think, "Please, make it stop!" It was surreal. I was numb. I felt like I was in a fog, unsure of my next step and frightened out of my mind. We can't be here. It's Monday. We should be at work. I knew in my heart something was very wrong.

My mind was racing as I tried to remember clues to what might have caused all this. Two weeks prior, something had happened to

Daryle at work. He was a driver for a uniform company. He had done this type of work pretty much most of our married life. I recalled that on this particular day, he had struggled to carry a large load of uniforms, hangers, and mats into one of the businesses. He suddenly tripped, and down he went. He smacked the back of his head on the hard cement floor and ended up with a terrible headache and a knot the size of an egg! Happy that no one had seen his graceful flight to the floor, he kept on with his daily schedule, and only mentioned the fall to me later that night at dinner. I asked if he was in any pain and felt the huge bump on the back of his head, but he reassured me, "I'll be okay, honey. Don't worry." Daryle had faith and I was a woman of faith, but now things weren't okay. Many times during the extensive examination, I felt as if I were going under. I couldn't understand why any of this was happening, but I believed God's word, "And we know that in all things God works for the good of those who love him, who have been called according to his purpose" (Romans 8:28, NIV), even though I couldn't possibly imagine how God could use this situation to do that.

Things moved quickly. We passed through a tempest of doctors explaining terms like "lesions," "mass," and "tumors." A top neurosurgeon was called in and Daryle was shuffled from test to test. We were all asked to wait in a cubicle of a room with a dingy, stained curtain for what seemed like hours. My husband's constant words to me as he grabbed my hands and looked into my bloodshot, tear-soaked eyes were, "Don't worry. I'm not going anywhere!" Despite his assurances, I was walking through a waking nightmare in fear. I did not yet have Daryle's confident faith. I felt like I was living someone else's life, as if I were peering through a window at someone else's troubles and suffering. I was filled with compassion, even though the life before me was my own. Reality slapped me back into focus as I heard, "Brain surgery is the only way to make a proper diagnosis." I cried uncontrollably. I dry-heaved and had to step out into the fresh air to keep from passing out. Our reality had just changed forever.

My body was literally buzzing. I had just watched the specialist review brain scans across the hall as he unconsciously shook his head in dismay. I hoped they weren't Daryle's. Unfortunately, the doctor's next stop was Room 7, at Daryle's bedside. I knew God's Word says, "Do not be anxious about anything, but in every situation, by prayer and petition, with thanksgiving, present your requests to God." (Philippians 4:6, NIV) Well, I can tell you the Lord heard a lot from me that day. I found this to be an extremely challenging scripture. I mean, really, "Don't be anxious?" Waves were crashing all around me. I felt as if I could barely breathe, yet even during all the chaos, deep within my heart I did experience a strange calming peace at the height of this storm. If not for God's loving care for me along with the wonderful support of my family, my church family and friends, I don't know what would have happened to me as we waited for the results.

My phone rang off the hook. Eventually I made the call to Daryle's boss who was utterly shocked. He explained that his brother was going through the same thing, and that his thoughts and prayers were with us. I then realized I had to call Darlene, Daryle's mom. This was a phone call I did not want to have to make. My thoughts raced, "I can't make this call. How is this possible? This is not happening! Wake me up! Jesus, help me!"

CHAPTER 2

THE BACKSTORY

My husband Daryle Wayne Borrows was born 8 lbs. 8 oz. in Williston, North Dakota, on July 2, 1959. He came into this world through one mom and was lovingly given to another. Darlene was an expectant mother. She already had a five-year-old daughter and found herself in circumstances where she knew she would not be able to care for her new baby as she wanted to. Darlene met the Borrows' in church. They were travelling as evangelists and had set up camp in North Dakota for a few months. In this time Darlene got to know them well, and learned that Reverend Bill and Lil Borrows were desperate to have children. Lil had had four miscarriages, and Darlene was comforted with the hope that the Borrows might want to adopt her precious child. All eventually agreed that the Borrows would adopt Darlene's baby, and Daryle's new life was set in motion.

Darlene wrote many letters to the Borrows' as her due date approached and, thankfully many years later, I discovered them tucked away in an old shoebox, along with the official papers pertaining to the adoption. The Borrows legally adopted Daryle and received him directly from the hospital at just three days old. The Borrows named him Daryle because it was the closest they could come to matching his mom's name. They hoped this would in some way preserve his connection to her. Darlene later shared that the Borrows brought him to visit her when he was just a month old. They informed her that Bill was looking for work and that they'd decided to move away to Fremont, California. Though saddened, Darlene understood and kissed her baby boy goodbye, expecting that she would never see him again. Daryle was around eight years old when his parents finally told him that he was adopted. They feared that he would respond negatively or that he might feel differently towards them, but Daryle simply said, "Cool. Okay." He didn't quite understand what it all meant, but he was happy. Daryle was part of a tradition. Bill had also been adopted at the age of four by the Borrows, a Canadian family. Daryle and his dad had a profound bond because of this.

California was beautiful, but finding work as a minister was hard, so Bill had to take whatever work he could find to support his family. His friend offered him a job as a carpenter. Bill had no experience as a carpenter but wasn't afraid of the challenge because he had done many other odd jobs. Ironically, God orchestrated this to provide Bill with the skills he would need to build a church years later. Daryle's mom, Lil Borrows, was a bright and devoted homemaker who had the biggest heart of anyone I have ever known. She loved her family and shared her love with anyone who crossed her path. Daryle was a healthy, normal little boy in every way, blessed with two loving parents.

Bill Borrows happily settled in California and eventually did become a local preacher, but in 1969 he felt God call him to the New England area. After many inquiries, the district superintendent of the

Assemblies of God in Massachusetts, Reverend David Flower, told him, "Come on down. We have a church for you." Bill and Lil sold all they had and bought a 13-foot white Shasta trailer, hitched it to the back of their 1968 green Mercury, and began the long journey across the United States via a stop in Canada to visit family. (Daryle later totaled their beloved Mercury in his teen years. When asked what happened, he spouted, "I was daydreaming about Suzie!")

Back to 1969: Daryle was ten years old and about to enjoy the greatest adventure of his life on a 3,000-mile cross-country camping trip. It took them approximately two months to complete the trek. Their excitement grew as they drew near to the place where they would finally put down roots to serve the Lord. New Bedford, Massachusetts, their new home, was a very different place from Fremont, California. As they pulled up to the church building, disappointment overwhelmed their hearts. They had thought for sure that they would be coming to worship in a grand building. But when they arrived, Daryle thought it was a warehouse. Bill remembered that God had spoken to his heart one Sunday evening after a poorly attended service, saying that He was going to "open a bigger door," but Bill thought this couldn't possibly be it. Believing that it must only be the beginning of something better and knowing that God had called him here, he simply said, "Okay, God. Let's do it." So began their new life in New Bedford.

Daryle started elementary school at the Mount Pleasant Street School and, unbeknownst to us, we were both attending the school at the same time. I had only been there for a year after returning from Ireland with my parents. I was just a little first grader who was picked on because of my Irish accent, and Daryle was a shy quiet boy in the fifth grade. He often said he wished he had met me back then. In any case, the Lord was connecting us in ways we wouldn't even realize for years to come. Daryle was very athletic and soon began playing hockey, basketball, and little league baseball. As a teenager, he eventually joined the church softball league. He also enjoyed learning the guitar and the piano, for which he won an award from the city at a very young age. God gave him a gift, which he used from his teen years on to worship God and to lead others to worship the Lord with him.

Daryle was a product of his mother's faith. Lil was an extraordinary woman. Though small physically (barely five feet tall), she was a woman of enormous faith and determination. By 1972 she realized that the congregation was starting to outgrow the church they'd built at the beginning of their ministry, so they started to look for a site to build a new church. Lil was resourceful and bold. She found a property and, with only $60 dollars in the bank, they purchased 818 Church Street to build their new church home. The plans were drawn and Reverend Bill Borrows became chief architect and builder. Construction went on for two years. It was truly a labor of love by Bill and many of the congregation who shed blood, sweat, and tears to create the uniquely shaped building. Onlookers often wondered if they were building a church or an ark!

Daryle and his friends used to have fun teasing his dad during the building process. Boys will be boys, even PK's (Preacher's kids). Daryle once told me that he and his friend Eli would throw snowballs over the roof of the church in the hope that they would roll down the other side onto some unsuspecting worker. His dad got quite annoyed and yelled at the boys to quit it. But of course one more snowball just had to fly, and Eli's ball hit Pastor Bill squarely on top of his bald head! A perfect shot! His dad came running around with a hammer in his hand and the boys took off. Another time, Daryle laughingly recalled how he and Eli would sit in the rafters shooting spitballs onto the working congregation! Though these pranks were less than admirable, they demonstrated the spirit of joy and freedom that filled the Borrows' hearts, home, and church life.

Daryle's mom and dad dedicated the rest of their lives to the newly named Christian Fellowship Center (CFC). Bill thought that name sounded contemporary and had a better chance of reaching the younger crowd, which it did. Adjacent to the church was a single-family home, and that is where Daryle and his parents lived. They held services in the basement of their home until construction of the new church was completed. Oh happy, happy days! This new building is where I finally met Daryle and where we all settled in as one big happy church family. These were wonderful years that witnessed our marriage, the birth of our children, and nineteen wonderful years where God allowed me to work as my father-in-law's secretary. I grew a lot there. And we all grew together. We truly felt a sense of fellowship and pride working for the Lord and serving His people.

Years passed as we experienced the same joys and struggles as other people. One of the hardships we faced was the loss of Lil, who passed away in July of 1996. When she died, I lost my best friend, Daryle lost his adoring mother, and Bill lost the love of his life, his prayer warrior and ministry partner. They'd been married for forty-six years. Witnessing this loss and its devastating impact on Bill was my introduction to the deep sorrow and grief that comes from losing your soul mate. Bill lived with us for five years until he too passed away in December of 2001.

After his passing, we realized that just as the former president's kids don't remain in the White House, we could no longer remain in at CFC. So with heavy hearts we left the church home we'd enjoyed for over thirty years. Eventually the building Bill had so lovingly built in the early 70s was torn down to make way for improvements to the church. Our sadness was tempered by a sense that this was the fulfillment of the Lord's promise to Bill all those years ago to give him a "bigger door." Though Lil and Bill did not get to see the realization of that dream, their dedication and hard work provided a beautiful foundation for the preaching of God's Word and the reaching of many people.

Bill's life and faith helped form the man Daryle grew to be. Bill's faith had been tested and was real. His solid faith was something he lived by and imparted to his son. I can remember Bill, or Dad as I called him, telling me stories of his early Christian life as a young man. He shared that in his day and age, going bowling was a sin! I suspect that growing up in the 30s and 40s must have been quite a challenge for young Christian adults. That may be why he walked away from his faith, joined the army, and lived a very non-Christian lifestyle before the Lord began to call him back. One day while Bill was on leave, he was out drinking with a buddy. On their way back to the barracks, they were involved in a terrible accident. His friend lost his life and Dad was ejected halfway out of the vehicle. He broke his leg, and his face and nose were partly torn off. He ended up with well over a hundred stitches to repair his nose, face, chin, and tongue.

You would think this life-threatening experience would have been a sufficient wake-up call. Unfortunately, it took another few years for him to rededicate his life to the Lord, but by 1947, he was a changed man. How good and patient is our God! He is not willing that any should perish. God's longsuffering heart toward Bill transformed him. And God used Bill's suffering to make him an especially compassionate pastor and shepherd to the lost.

After committing his life to Christ, Dad headed off to Bible

College, where he met Lil Esther Amber Stanley. Lil was always proud of the fact that her family line included the famous Lord Stanley who established the national hockey league in Canada, her native country. Anyway, Lil wanted nothing to do with Bill, but he kept telling her he would marry her one day. Her response was, "Ha! That will be the day. Keep dreaming, Bill!" Lil wanted to be a missionary to China and *not* marry, but the Lord had other plans for her! Isn't it funny how one decision can change the course of our lives? It struck me that if she had done what she'd wanted, my Daryle wouldn't be mine! I'm so happy she chose to cooperate with God! Well, a few years later the wedding bells did ring, and a new life began for Bill and Lil. They worked hard as ministers of the gospel and lived in many different places. They even ministered on an Indian reservation, which Lil loved. I think she could have lived there forever, but God led them onward.

Though life and people were not always kind to them, God preserved them. I remember one particular story they often told about a congregation that was "stuck" in their old ways of thinking. They wanted to get rid of Dad and his recommended reforms. One day he went to the church and found it chained shut! They refused to pay him and literally tried to starve them out! Lil mentioned to me that their diet consisted of eating peas on toast and a lot of bologna.

Thankfully the Lord was with them and moved them into evangelistic work in a little Wild West one-horse town called Tioga, North Dakota. Here they ministered at Reverend Strom's church, Tioga Assembly of God. The Lord truly heard the cries of their aching hearts to have a child, for this is where they met Darlene. It was in this very town years before that Daryle's grandmother, Inga, had met the Borrows. It was Inga who connected them to Darlene and her unborn baby. Inga was a prayerful woman who knew it would be best to find a Christian home for her future grandchild and helped facilitate the adoption. Even so, she grieved at the thought of never seeing him again. But when Daryle was eight months old, Bill wrote a sweet letter to Inga as if Daryle had written it himself, telling her all about his young life thus far. After that precious event, communication ceased as their lives moved in different directions.

Because Tioga was so important to Daryle's story, he and I visited the town more than once. Each time it felt like we'd gone back to the 1800s. The layout and design looked exactly like a Hollywood set, and you could see for miles in every direction. There was only one stoplight, and no one locked their doors. During one visit, we walked into a restaurant to have breakfast. To our surprise, everyone stopped eating and turned their eyes towards us just like a bar room scene from an old Western because clearly, they weren't used to seeing strangers in "them thar" parts. Miraculously, Inga was reunited with Daryle soon before her own death at ninety-eight years old.

CHAPTER 3

FAMILY TIES

Darlene came back into Daryle's life when he was thirty-five years old, prompted by a song by Bruce Carroll he had heard called, "Sometimes When We Love." It's a song about a mother searching for the child she gave up at birth. This song made him wonder if Darlene was curious about him. Every year on his birthday I would ask, "Do you want to try to find her?" His reply was always, "I'm okay, honey."

But this time it was different. He decided, "Let's try to find her." We talked to his parents who were on board, so the search began. God was alive and active in our midst. Sometimes people search for years but we were reconnected the very next day. Dad called the same little church in Tioga that they had visited thirty-five years earlier. The same pastor was still there, and he knew that Daryle's grandmother was in a little nursing home not far from the church. He gave us the phone number and, as our hearts raced, Daryle placed the call. Darlene's sister-in-law, who just "happened" to be visiting at that very moment, answered the phone. Daryle explained who he was. She said, "Wow, Darlene will be very surprised to hear this news."

We exchanged all our contact info immediately. We had Darlene's name, address, and phone, and she now had his. We learned that he had three other siblings, and they all lived near Denver, Colorado. Hoping to reunite, my husband wrote a beautiful letter to his mother on March 8, 1995, and we waited to hear back. Daryle was very anxious because it took a long time for her to respond, but I kept telling him, "Honey, you don't know what she is going through right now. Just give her a little time."

Finally, a letter appeared in our mailbox on April 24. I'd run downstairs to get the mail as I always did and saw Darlene's name on the envelope. My heart jumped. I immediately called my husband at work and said, "Guess what I'm holding?" He was beyond excited. The second he walked through the door, I handed it to him. We sat and read it together with tears in our eyes. He was so happy that he'd reached out to her and that she was not upset about being contacted by the son she'd given up. She mentioned that she had just seen a movie about a mom searching for her adopted child and it got her thinking about Daryle once more. How incredible that just as Daryle heard a song, his mother watched a movie that caused them to long for each other.

It was amazing to see God's hand in the timing of events, both in reuniting their hearts and at the same time providing a way to reunite them physically. Three days before Daryle's letter, her husband (not Daryle's birth father) had had a stroke and passed away. Though life had so drastically and tragically changed for Darlene, she was now free to travel from Colorado to New Bedford, which is just what she did in October of 1995. The rest is history as they say.

This visit created an instant bond. The ties between mother and child had not been broken by time and distance. We celebrated an even larger family reunion that February when we brought our children to

Colorado to meet all of Daryle's biological family, and it has been wonderful ever since.

Back to 2012.... I needed to make the phone call to Darlene. I dreaded the thought of telling her that she might lose the son that she had been united with at last. I could hardly get the words out, but Darlene was very calm. She reassured me that Daryle would be okay, and that she and his brother Todd would make a trip out to us as soon as they could. Meanwhile, I went back in and told Daryle what she'd said. Even in his condition, he was more concerned for her state of mind and well-being (she was in her late seventies) than he was for his own.

Another phone call I did not want to make was to Daryle's sister Mary, his sibling on his biological father's side. "Stan the Music Man" as he was known in Ray, North Dakota, was the father of Mary, Jerome, and Daryle. Mary and Jerome had only recently learned that Daryle existed and were hoping to meet him, but before they could, Jerome died of colon cancer at just thirty-seven years old. Daryle and Mary are only nine months apart and though Mary had lost one brother, she was about to gain another.

They finally met on July 4, 1998 in Seattle, Washington. The long-awaited reunion was filmed by The Learning Channel on a show called "Reunion." It was also a front-page story in our local paper, *The Standard Times*. Mary already experienced so much loss by the time she met Daryle that finding him was huge. We also got to meet Stan. Daryle and Mary were together by his side before he too passed away from cancer. As brother and sister, they both witnessed to Stan and were blessed to see him accept Jesus before he passed. Sharing the moment of their father's salvation cemented their relationship. It was an incredible time in our lives. Daryle went from basically no family to an explosion of loving relatives.

Mary subsequently within a few months moved across country from Seattle with her two daughters, Dana and Kaitlyn, to New Bedford, to be nearer to Daryle, our son Rick, our daughter Stephanie, and me. We all became very close. Mary felt that he was her gift from God. She said that knowing Daryle made coffee taste better and rain smell sweeter. Having lost her mother, brother and father, we became her family. The powerful bond between Mary and Daryle made hearing the news about his condition even more difficult, but it drove us all to pray like never before.

Back at St. Luke's Hospital, the neurosurgeon finally came to meet with the whole family. He explained that the only way he could determine the actual cause of Daryle's symptoms was to perform a craniotomy to retrieve a piece of his brain to send to pathology. I knew right then we were in for a long haul. On the day of the surgery, I remember the hard cold look of the steel gurney as it was wheeled into the room to take Daryle to the operating room. I thought, "What if he doesn't survive?" I was trembling from the fear that was gripping every part of my being. I splashed some smelly chlorinated water on a facecloth and tried to hide the fact that I was dry-heaving in his private bathroom. I came out and hugged and kissed him when he said again, with absolute certainty, "I'm not going anywhere." I nodded with swollen eyes and tear-stained cheeks and said, "Okay, love." He told me later that he'd heard my sobbing and never wanted to hear me in that much pain ever again! Despite everything he faced, he was more concerned for me than for himself.

The surgeon came in prior to surgery to explain, "I like to follow the hairline when I do brain surgery, so it won't be as noticeable as it heals. Daryle has a very long hairline." Daryle was conscious and hadn't lost his sense of humor. He replied, "Well, sorry, Doc. I've always had a big head!" That broke the tension for a second.

As they wheeled him away, I lay down in Daryle's hospital bed trying to nestle into the impression of his body on the mattress in an attempt to stay as close to him as possible. I was slammed with the reality that my husband might not return! My sister Tracey (we call her Tra, pronounced Tray) and Pastor John (our pastor at the time) tried to console me. I was curled up in a fetal position as my mind explored every deadly "what if" known to man. I didn't know if he was going to come back to me. Could I lose him? Is this the day? If he comes back, how much damage will they have done? Will he know me? The doctors had explained that anything could happen and if they accidentally hit the wrong part of the brain, his loss would be irretrievable. I was shaken!

My beliefs, my faith, my understanding, my future hopes, my dreams were all shaken. No one could rationally speak to my fears. I wanted and needed to hear the Lord's voice. The well-intentioned words of those around me fell like lead balls to the icy tiled floor. I thought to myself, and actually said out loud, "I don't want to hurt your feelings, but please stop talking!" I didn't want to hear anything they had to say. When you are in the depths, people who care desperately want to help you, but it always feels like you are in the depths alone. I knew no human could make a difference … only God.

The rest of the family was with me, except for our son Rick who lived in upstate New York. We were keeping him informed with daily updates. As we waited, I kept pacing while my heart kept pounding. The surgery was only supposed to take an hour, but we entered a second hour, and then a third. I thought I was going to get sick! But then we got the call that they'd sent him upstairs to the CICU (critical intensive care unit). Walking to the elevator to get to him seemed to take forever. My mind was swirling, "Is he in pain? Did they shave his head? Did they get it all? Did they make any mistakes?" I felt nauseous. I just wanted to be with him. I wanted to hold his hand, but two very heavy large doors protected the CICU. The only way to get in was to be buzzed in. It only holds about ten patients at a time. I was terrified because he wasn't only in "Intensive Care," he was actually "critical," i.e. in a life-threatening state. I was also relieved because I knew at the very least that they closely monitored him 24/7.

As I rounded the corner, I caught a glimpse of Daryle. He was a mess. There were wires, drainage hoses, dried blood, and a very large white cotton gauze bandage firmly wrapped around his head. Once peeled back, it revealed a large incision that shocked me. It went from the top of his head to the front of his ear. It was thick, and he had approximately thirty surgical steel staples attached to his skull. Thankfully the surgery was a success, and they were able to retrieve a piece of the tumor. Unfortunately, the doctor informed us that the rest was just too deep in the brain and they risked serious injury if they went after it.

On top of all the challenges we already faced, Stephanie was interning at St. Luke's Hospital at the same time that Daryle was undergoing surgery and treatment there. She was studying in the hospital program to become a registered dietitian. Her dad was now her patient in the CICU. Thankfully the administration gave her the option to assign someone else to her dad's care, which she gratefully accepted. They were so kind that they even gave her time off in the midst of finals. We witnessed how miraculously God moves in the hearts of people. This was just one of the many kindnesses we experienced at St. Luke's.

Daryle received the absolute best treatment there! Everyone took exceptional care of him. From the doctors to the staff who cleaned his room, each person took an interest in his well-being. Their concern for him helped me so much because I was emotionally spent. From the get-go they treated him like family, doing their best to make sure he was comfortable and taking care of his every need. Recovering in the CICU after surgery, the morphine flowed steadily to keep his pain down and to keep him calm.

Despite all the love and care surrounding Daryle, I felt terribly alone and frightened. Amazingly, our friend Sue worked in the hospital during Daryle's stay. She was a great comfort to me. No one could get into the CICU unless you were family or worked there, so she routinely checked in on Daryle. One day she stopped by just as the assistant surgeon came in to tell us that it would be a few days before pathology could give us any results, and that if radiation or chemotherapy were needed, they would contact me. Now I'm no rocket scientist, but in my mind you wouldn't say those words unless you had reason to believe that the diagnosis was cancer. From the very beginning of Daryle's ordeal, no one had spoken the "C" word, but Sue just hugged me and in my heart I knew. We looked at each other and cried. For me, this was the second longest day.

By this time, I knew that Daryle was resting quietly and that he was in good hands. I realized I needed some rest too. After three days with almost no sleep, I finally drove the 25 minutes back home but instead of curling up for a power nap, I quickly threw in some laundry and cried, and cried, and cried. I had barely taken my coat off when my phone rang.

"Yes?"

"Mrs. Borrows. This is the nurse in the CICU. Your husband has become a bit combative and has ripped off his bandage four or five times and is asking for you."

Seriously? Oh, my gosh!

"Okay, please tell him I'm coming."

With adrenaline pumping, I drove right back to the hospital and walked into the room to find him pulling at his head again.

He said, "There is something on my head and they won't let me take it off."

I lovingly took his hands and said, "Honey, look into my eyes." He did and I said, "Do you trust me?"

"Well, yeah, honey, I trust you."

"Then please leave the bandage alone. It needs to stay a little longer to heal. And I will be with you."

"Okay, but I don't understand."

I couldn't understand why he didn't understand. Was it because of the drugs? Did they take out his "understand button"? What was wrong?

This was a man who wrote music! He was so stinking smart. How could someone who had the intelligence to handle the complexity of composing original songs, organizing an entire worship team, and arranging all the instruments suddenly be reduced to a toddler trying to rip a bandage off his boo boo? My heart was breaking for him as we waited by his side day in and day out, hoping that his status would be downgraded and that the bandage would come off. His mind was fuzzy and the operation caused tremors, but the day finally came when, yay, we were moved to another floor! Progress! Daryle was moved to the second floor. Both my mom (a nurse for thirty years at this hospital) and my daughter (interning there) knew what that meant, but I was oblivious and just happy to get out of CICU.

I found out later the second floor is the cancer floor. This just made me angry. We still hadn't even been told that he had cancer. The pathology report hadn't even come back yet, so why would they put him there? In my mind I was trying to put the pieces together, but in an effort to help my faith triumph, I denied the obvious. Every time I walked onto that floor, I just started to boldly pray for the people in the rooms. I prayed that they would be healed in Jesus' name, and "Oh yeah, Lord, don't forget about 'my Cheese' in the last room." In the midst of this sterile environment and this emotional agony, my pet name for Daryle brought some lightness to the heaviness of everything we were going through. It made me feel "normal." "Cheese" was a nickname I lovingly gave him after a childhood song we both knew. A friend of mine even stopped by my house to deliver a t-shirt she'd created for me with "I love my Cheese" appliqued in colored rhinestones. Soon everybody in the hospital started referring to him as "my Cheese."

The second floor ended up being a great place for Daryle to recuperate. He was originally in a room with a man who coughed relentlessly. The coughing actually gave Daryle headaches, so the nurses decided to move him to a large room by himself. The grand window in Daryle's room now afforded a full view of the front of the hospital, and he could see who was coming and going. Countless people came to visit, to share hope and to pray for him. They were hurting too, but we all stood together in faith believing. We were a faith couple, a faith family, a faith church! We believed we would win this *because* we *believed*!

Our church family at the time was very supportive. They brought meals, sent cards, and prayed their hearts out. Daryle's illness was a big blow to the church. Daryle was the worship leader and a father figure to many kids who didn't have a dad at home. We had always taken kids for trips: to the beach, roller-skating, bike riding, for ice cream, and anything else that was needed. He was also a deacon, an elder, and friend to the pastor. I was the pastor's secretary. We were a close-knit group and enjoyed real love in the church. Pastor John was a true blessing to us in this dark time, spending countless hours with us and aiding us in any way possible as we waited to see God's hand move miraculously in Daryle's life.

CHAPTER 4

The Hard Road

The definition of "hard" is "requiring a great deal of endurance and effort." Many people comforted us through the surgery, but "treatment" is a long road you walk alone. You struggle through medications up the wazoo, blood thinners, antibiotics, and pain meds. You name it, he had it. From the day of surgery onward, Daryle suffered continuously from tremors. Thankfully he could eat with no problem, so he did, and I was happy to give him whatever he wanted. As we settled into a routine at the hospital, we did try some alternative methods such as juicing and special cancer diets to see if they would help, but we did not see any change.

One sunlit day I ran up to get something that we'd forgotten in the CICU and literally bumped into the neurosurgeon as we rounded corners. He was looking for Daryle. I said, "Oh, they moved him downstairs a couple of days ago." He was happy to hear it, and then he put his arm around my shoulder and said, "Walk with me."

"Okay," I said.

Then he asked me, "How are you coping with all of this?"

With a shrug, I replied, "I am only strong because God only gives me manageable doses that I can handle."

As we walked, we entered a little sitting room at the end of the hall. No one was in there but us. I could hear myself having a separate conversation with him in my head and finally had the courage to ask the tough question. I gathered up my strength and said, "Doctor. I don't want the red tape, I don't want pathology. I don't want the waiting. I want the truth."

Knowing that he performed this surgery a thousand times before, I believed that he knew it was cancer. He looked down at the floor. I could see him contemplating whether or not to divulge that information, but pleading my case, I explained that I wanted and needed time to "digest" whatever he told me before everyone else knew. He looked right into my eyes and said, "You are a strong person, Suzie. Yes, it is cancer."

I proceeded to tell the doctor how surreal everything felt. "We're not supposed to be here. We were planning to take the boat and go fishing on Memorial Day. We had a bet on who would catch the biggest fish!"

He laughed and kindly told me that I should not worry and to keep doing what I was doing, promising by the summer I would be fishing again. He had given me hope. I wasn't quite sure if the doctor believed his own words, but I went with it.

I decided to tell Daryle what the doctor said. His response was, "No worries, love. God will take care of me." People all over the world were praying for Daryle, but only he and I knew the truth. For a moment, we were alone with God facing a frightening future, but His Word declares "Even in darkness light dawns for the upright, for those who are gracious and compassionate and righteous. Good will come to those who are generous and lend freely, who conduct their affairs with justice. Surely the righteous will never be shaken; they will be remembered forever. They will have no fear of bad news; their hearts are steadfast, trusting in the Lord." (Psalm 112:4–7, NIV)

Despite the mountain in front of us, the surgeon had encouraged us with the dream of a summer fishing trip. You know, hope in its smallest form is a wonderful thing. The Bible states that "hope deferred makes the heart sick, but a dream fulfilled is a tree of life." (Proverbs 13:12, NIV) Wow. I was starting to cling to God's Word like I never had before. What a comfort to my heart it had become. My mind kept going back to scriptures the Lord had given my husband two years prior in May of 2010. He was sleeping and heard the Lord call his name. It was around 3:00 a.m. He got up and went to his office and said, "Yes Lord, what did you want to say?" He grabbed his Bible and the Lord took him to these scriptures:

1. "I will sing and make music to the Lord." (Psalm 27:6, NIV)
2. "Unless the Lord builds the house, its builders labor in vain." (Psalm 127:1, NIV)
3. "Sing praises to God, Sing praises; Sing praises to our King, Sing praises!" (Psalm 47:6, NLT)
4. "The Lord sustains them on their sickbed and restores them from their bed of illness." (Psalm 41:3, NIV)
5. "I will praise You, Lord, with all my heart; before the 'gods' I will sing Your praise." (Psalm 138:1, NIV)
6. "When I called, You answered me; you made me bold and stouthearted." (Psalm 138:3, NIV)
7. "The LORD will fulfill His purpose for me; Your steadfast

love, O LORD, endures forever. Do not forsake the work of Your hands." (Psalm 138:8, ESV)

8. "Wait for the LORD; be strong and take heart and wait for the LORD." (Psalm 27:14, ESV)
9. "They will still bear fruit in old age, they will stay fresh and green." (Psalm 92:14, NIV)

Needless to say, when I awoke that day in May, he came in and told me what happened and showed me the scriptures. I immediately vetoed number four and said, "What, are you going to get pneumonia or something?" That was the worst thing I could think of.

He said, "Well, honey, whatever I get, the Lord would restore me from it."

Yikes! "Okay, love."

Life went on, and we had not really thought of those scriptures for years until suddenly they came back to our minds front and center, especially number four! I kept reminding Daryle of the promise that God would sustain and restore him. I kept reminding myself of the promise. This was no pneumonia! I knew this event did not shake God off the throne. He knew it was coming.

Finally, the day came when we were able to go home. Oh, happy day! I created copies of those scripture verses and plastered them everywhere in the house. We declared God's Word constantly. We even took a baseball hat and wrote these scriptures in permanent ink inside the cap. Daryle proudly wore it all that day and night. When he removed the hat, to our surprise, the writing was tattooed on top of his head! After a few chuckles and much scrubbing, we determined we should just keep them on the walls!

I expected Daryle to heal better at home, surrounded by family, friends, and familiar things. His special joy was seeing Lily and Jack, our niece's children. It's amazing how these little ones lifted his spirits. I also thanked God for my parents. They lived next door separated only by a small bridge over the pond connecting our properties. We would have been lost without them. They were the constant source of help and encouragement Daryle and I needed. They took turns sitting with him, giving me a reprieve to run out for groceries or to work for a couple of hours. Their presence allowed me to keep some semblance of normalcy which I desperately needed.

The community rallied around us as well. I was so grateful for all the love and help. But one day I received a phone call from someone we hadn't heard from in years. Hoping for a word of encouragement, I was met instead with the words, "If you give Daryle chemotherapy, you might as well put a nail in his coffin." Why thank you, sister sandpaper! People often don't realize how what they say can wound others. My mother used to teach us, "If you can't say anything nice, don't say anything at all." I think that rule definitely applies when someone is struggling or fighting for their lives!

We knew by this time Daryle would never work again, making our growing financial burden even more frightful. To add insult to injury, we received a $2,000 bill from the hospital charging us for the room change that the nurses had decided on! Why must everything be a fight? We won that one, praise God! We'd faced this kind of trouble and God had done miracles for us before. Back in our younger days, around October of 1986 Daryle was sick of driving a truck and decided to change his occupation … to become a used car salesman. Oh, boy! Our son Rick was almost three and Steph was just a few weeks old. Our rent at the time was $80 a week, which was a lot then, never mind diapers. It seemed obvious that this job would not pay our bills, not to mention it did not suit Daryle's personality. He was a man of integrity, and they wanted him to lie to the customers. He refused and, as result, he did not sell many cars. That meant no money coming in. Many paychecks were only $60, not even enough to cover the rent.

The stress started building. I began to fall into a depression, barely doing anything around the house, though I did care for the children since that was about all I could muster. Our relationship was strained because I was so stressed, and he was so frustrated. He was given a loaner car, a grey station wagon, but was supposed to sell it after a specified time. If he failed, they would not give him another one. Well, two cars were a big help for us, but more stress knowing that it was a gift with huge strings attached.

After months of financial and emotional pressure, I cried myself to sleep telling the Lord that I just couldn't handle anymore. I felt like giving up. That night I had an amazing, life-changing dream. I was standing in our kitchen talking on the phone to my mom. I hung up and turned around. Standing there was the hugest angel. Our ceilings were nine feet and he almost hit them. I immediately fell to my knees and thought, "Oh boy, I've done it now!" He was covered in white flowing material. He had dark hair and a strong jaw, and it looked to me like he had a little tan. He put his gigantic hand on my head. His pinky finger was on one temple and his thumb covered the other temple, just as you might caress a little kitten. I remember thinking, "Wow, he could crush me!" He then spoke, "Do not be afraid. The Lord has sent me to tell you, my child, not to worry. All things will be okay." I felt like more was to be revealed, like there was something yet unknown, but I had no idea what it was. I replied, "Thank you." As I looked up, he was gone.

I awoke the next morning and it took me a few moments to process my dream, but wow, I felt like the energizer bunny! I knew that I had been healed of my depression overnight. I knew that God had heard me and answered me. It was going to be okay. Daryle on the other hand was skeptical and showed little faith at that time. It was his last chance. The car had to sell by the end of the day or he would lose it. He reminded me, "You know this is it—the last day." I told him that God would work it all out and that I would be at his mom's house. I asked him to call me when God sold the car.

Daryle replied, "Okay, but . . . ."

"No buts!" I said. "Call me at your mom's!"

An hour later, the phone rang. I bellowed, "I'll get it!" As I lifted the receiver, I said, "Hi, honey."

"How did you know it was me?"

"I told you God told me the car would sell and I expected it to happen, so tell me?"

In a sheepish voice he conveyed, "Yes, I sold the car."

I retorted, "Who sold the car?"

"God sold the car."

Talk about excited! You couldn't hold me down. He sold three more that day!

A couple of days later he was sitting up in bed as I cozied up to my pillow, and he said, "Maybe that was a coincidence?"

I bolted up, "Are you kidding me? Well, that's okay, honey. God knows you so well He knew you would say that, so He showed me who you sold the car to in my dream."

Daryle sat up, crossed his arms, and shook his head, saying, "Oh, this I've got to hear!"

"Well, I don't know their names, but I can describe the scene. They are an older couple. He is wearing a tan trench coat, and she has a blue one on. He is so tall you are telling him to be careful not to hit his head. He is on the right side of your desk. She is on the left and he has a cane." Daryle's mouth dropped open.

"Honey, that is exactly who I sold the car to!"

It just bubbled out of me. I knew there was more to the dream. How I love the Lord, my ever-present help in time of trouble! Thankfully the car-selling days were short-lived, and Daryle was back to what he knew best.

Thinking back to those times, I knew God would be with us in our present mess. As if collapse, surgery, cancer, hospital stays, and constant medicine weren't challenging enough, we exhausted our excellent insurance after only one month. This forced me to sift through page after page of healthcare info as I applied for state care. I had to make sure that whatever provider I picked for my husband would accept his radiologist, his oncologist, and his neurosurgeon, and that their offices would accept his new insurance. The process was tedious and exhausting. I just can't imagine elderly folks in a similar situation having to go through all of this, when it was so complicated and overwhelming for me.

Waiting at home, we were just anxious for good news and encouraging words. I recall several phone calls from a nurse whom we did not know who insisted that Daryle look into alternative medicine. After all that we'd had to endure thus far, the prospect of putting him in the car and driving to Texas completely overwhelmed me. I remember the suggestion had something to do with high doses of almonds and cyanide. Sensing my reluctance after her repeated phone calls, she finally said with quite the attitude, "Then Daryle will die!" and she hung up on me. I rejected her words and cried my eyes out. We were already dealing with trauma. How was this supposed to help?

From the outset, we agonized over what the best treatment would be and my "concerned" friend and this "helpful" nurse didn't help us in our distress at all. I remember just thinking they should give him something that would kill it! Why couldn't they just kill the monster growing inside him? I was so exhausted. I was visibly shaking from the stress. We were spending a lot of money beyond healthcare costs just to make sure he had everything he needed. We put new railings in our home. The church put in a special cement slab outside to make it easier to get in and out of the house with his wheelchair. My stepfather built an elevated platform to go underneath his recliner to make it easier for him to get his 6'2" frame up and out of the chair on his own. Honestly, we all happily did anything that would help him. Thank the Lord our family was so financially generous and helped us whenever we needed.

Even so, the weekly and monthly bills from doctors' visits were piling up. Invoices from Dana Farber Cancer Institute, radiation, chemotherapy, vascular, neurology, visiting nurses, occupational therapy, physical therapy, speech pathology just kept coming. It was nuts. I had to keep track of all the appointments, all the medications, all while being his intimate caretaker. To top it off, we were involved in a clinical trial with Dana Farber and had to answer multiple questions and fill out forms every day. Daryle could barely tell me if he wanted eggs for breakfast, let alone tell me his pain level on a scale of 1 to 10!

Much of Daryle's care came under the umbrella of hospice, but I didn't want "hospice" at first. I thought, what are they saying? That he's going to die? But my mom, the nurse, convinced me that it just opens the door for better services, so I reluctantly agreed. The hospice nurses were all very kind, but when they asked the tough question about signing the DNR (do not resuscitate), anger welled up in me and, with teeth clenched, I told the nurse not to ask me that again. I said, "Look at him!" (He had a cute, kissable smile on his face.) "Would you sign it?"

She replied, "No, I wouldn't."

Whether she was right or not, it made me feel better and I thanked her. Daryle knew what was at stake here, and my sweet hubby said, "Look at my woman go!" Our roles were changing, and he knew that I had become his protector. All I could think is, "I love that guy!"

I could feel myself buckling under the weight of my daily responsibilities and the many trials, crying out, "God, where are you? Do you hear us?" On the same day, Daryle and I both woke up feeling so discouraged and so very sad that we groaned together, "Please God, help."

About an hour later our friend Debbie stopped by. She proceeded to tell us that she was on a "God Errand" and that she had no intention of stopping by, but the Lord pressed her to do so. Her words to us were, "God sees how discouraged you are and knows you are in the valley, but one day you will have a mountaintop experience."

Well, my frame of mind wasn't exactly fabulous and I challenged her, "He sees, but is He really going to do anything about it?" I'm so glad God sees the bigger picture and doesn't smite us for the stupid things we say. He saw my hurting heart. We appreciated Deb's visit and the many times the Lord continued to use her to speak encouragement to our daughter and to us. Yet she often found me in a bad place, and she ended up bearing the brunt of my despair and fatigue. What a friend! She persevered anyway.

Despite the many difficulties, being home did ease my mind because I could be with Daryle constantly and accomplish simple, comforting tasks like laundry or making him breakfast. Due to the fact that the tumor was hitting parts of his brain that effected memory, he had trouble recalling what he had literally just said or whether he'd eaten, or who had been with him. Have you ever seen the movie *50 First Dates*? There you go.

I will never forget one day when I prepared his favorite breakfast. I gave it to him and was washing the dishes, but when I came back into the living room, I saw a priceless look on his face. I said, "What is it, honey?"

"Well, aren't we going to eat? It's already 9:30."

Honestly, I thought, "Are you kidding me? Lord, please help him!" I went right over to him and looked into his eyes and said, "Now don't get upset, honey, but think about your stomach at the moment. Does it feel full?"

"Nope! I could eat!"

"Okay, second breakfast it is!"

He had many seconds, and so did I! Thanks a lot, Daryle. I gained 20 pounds! Daryle asked the same questions over and over and we had to act like we'd never heard the question before so as to not hurt his feelings.

"How do I make a call on the cell phone? What day is it? Why have you been gone for hours?" when I'd only been away ten minutes. This was definitely a big change from our norm.

Our next challenge was dealing with the effect the tumor was having on Daryle's balance. He would get up to do something ordinary like grab the remote, but as he reached forward, his knees would buckle and down he would go. He had many falls, but he always remarked, "It's okay, love. Bumbles bounce."

Bumbles were the big snow monsters in our favorite Christmas Claymation movies like Rudolf and Frosty the Snowman. They would get pushed off a cliff and everyone would think, "Oh, that Bumble's dead." But then they would revive and holler "Bumbles bounce!" That was Daryle. You couldn't keep him down. Before his diagnosis, Daryle never took a sick day. He had been as healthy and strong as an ox.

But all that had changed. I will never forget the time Pastor John came to pick him up to take him to visit a homebound friend a couple of weeks later. I was a nervous wreck and didn't think he should go, but Daryle insisted he would be fine. Pastor reassured me that he would watch him. So, with my list in hand, I went shopping and they went visiting. A couple of hours later, I received a phone call from Daryle stating that they were on their way back, but he was okay.

"What do you mean 'okay,' honey?"

"Well, I lost my balance on the cement pavers between some sets of stairs, fell onto a short cement wall, and then slammed onto the concrete driveway."

I thought I was going to be sick! Poor Pastor John said, "He was right with me, and in a second he went down." Don't I know it! He fell many times under my watch, which I guess explains why I was so cautious about someone else caring for him. The huge purple, blue, and red bruises on his body convinced us that no matter how bored he was sitting at home, day trips without me were now out of the question.

My mind kept churning, "He is like a very large toddler: falling, tripping, struggling to get his words right, needing to be fed, and changed. This is my husband. How can this be happening? How else can I help him?" I was just so frustrated! Watching his daily struggles, it soon became apparent that there was simply no way he could keep climbing the stairs to our bedroom, so with the help of friends, I brought the bedroom downstairs to him. This made life a whole lot easier. I was no longer confident that I could completely trust him to be on his own. At this stage, I knew if he tried to go upstairs without assistance, he would fall. This way, when he was tired, he could just go lie down without much help.

CHAPTER 5

LITTLE VICTORIES

We did press on, and we did see many small victories and "improvements." The radiation was going well. The tumor was actually shrinking! He seemed to be getting better. We realized how blessed we were when we saw many others afflicted with greater challenges and more serious cancers. Amazingly, Daryle never got sick from chemotherapy as others do, but he decided to be proactive and shaved his head before the chemo even had a chance to take his hair. In solidarity, friends shaved their heads, including about twenty men from church and my sister who shaved a smidge of hers on the side. Daryle was so humbled and thankful for all the love and support.

Humor pops up in the weirdest places on the road to recovery. We all got a real chuckle one day after as Randy (my stepfather and Daryle's best friend) shaved his head. As he escorted Daryle by the arm out of the radiation center, a complete stranger tapped Randy and said, "Hang in there, buddy. We'll be praying for you," as if Randy were the patient, not Daryle. They thought that was hilarious and Daryle razzed Randy all day long. We were grateful for every little bit of joy and for every positive indication from the radiation treatments, and one of the greatest victories at that time was being allowed to take a weekend getaway together.

We couldn't make a move without the doctors' say so, but after getting clearance from them, we decided to take a little trip to Maine. Michelle's mom had a cabin on China Lake. It was something you would only see in a travel book. Majestic mountains, thickly forested with the smell of fresh pine, and a beautiful lake teeming with fish. It was perfect. My parents came with us and we actually did go fishing on the lake, just as the doctor promised many months before. We had a great time, and it was good to break away from our grueling routine. Due to the fact that it was a rustic cabin, the worn staircase was quite narrow. Daryle was crawling up the steps while we pushed him from behind. What a sight! We all needed a good laugh and that was it! Daryle enjoyed sitting in the creaky wooden rocking chair on the sun porch, staring out and marveling at God's many wonders.

When we returned home, Daryle was a bit stronger, so he actually went to church. Although he had to walk with a cane, he was able to sing "We Will Ride," one of the congregation's most loved songs. Daryle got a standing ovation from everyone. Normal seemed to be tiptoeing back into our lives. I remember thinking, "I could do this, Lord. If this is all we get, I can handle living like this. I'll take it."

After that trip, Daryle improved so much we couldn't believe it. We were excited for the first time in a long time. The victories kept coming. His numbers were all good. He had more energy. His conversation was more lucid. His memory seemed to be better. Our daughter, Stephanie, graduated from her internship and the hospital held a special dinner, which we were able to attend. Daryle felt great! Happy days!

Things seemed to be looking up, so much so that we booked a

Mediterranean cruise to Italy in September 2012 with our daughter and her husband. In our pre-cancer days, we had already cruised to the Caribbean and to Bermuda and had loved it. We would sit on our balconies enjoying the beautiful ocean and island views, feeling like we were in a dream. It was Heaven on earth. So, could it be possible again now? Could he really handle it now? He was doing so well and he wanted to go, so we dove into serious prayer, asking the Lord for guidance. We did not want to do the wrong thing or risk hurting Daryle in any way.

We knew we would need absolute clearance from every doctor. Amazingly, after meeting with all of them, they okayed our cruise! The top Dana Farber neurologist was so confident that we would be okay that he signed off and gave us the contact info for one of his colleagues in Italy just in case we needed help. This was a miracle. The most daunting issue facing us was how his brain would react to the change in air pressure at 30,000 feet. No one really knew. "Lord, should we do it?" We were still a bit concerned, but my hubby said, "No worries, love. Let's go!" Once again, my mind was racing. "Would this be our last trip? NO! I will not go there."

Stephanie and I went to the travel agent and made the arrangements. All four of us were so excited and felt like we had been given a great gift. We knew that this trip was significant not only because of Daryle's condition, but because the kids wanted to start a family and this was the last chance for them to travel before Steph would try to become pregnant. Great things were on the way. We just knew it.

About a month into all of our planning for our cruise, Daryle and I were sitting in the living room. We were talking when I noticed him turning his head back and forth towards the lamp beside him. He picked up his left arm and held it close to his chest. Confused, I asked, "Is there something wrong with the lamp, honey?"

He replied, "I can't make it stop."

I immediately called his doctor at Dana Farber and they knew right away. Seizures! "NO! Jesus!"

Now over 7,000 milligrams of anti-seizure meds were added to his daily routine, but the meds couldn't even fully stop the attacks. Our hope and dream of the perfect getaway was shattered. We encouraged the kids to go anyway, to have a great time and to make babies! It was a hard blow for us all, but not a knockout punch, and we carried on.

Though the seizures killed our plans to travel, we were still trying to make light of it and to find humor in the difficult things. Daryle hated the seizures, but they happened so often we all came to recognize the sign that he was about to have one. Daryle would turn his head and cross his arm over his chest like the Pledge of Allegiance. He was actually conscious during these episodes, and could speak to us, but he couldn't physically move and his limbs were completely frozen in place. One day he declared, "I just I hate this!"

Wanting to comfort her dad and knowing he was a WWII aficionado, Steph joked, "Well, Dad, it could be worse. Your arm could go straight out like Heil Hitler!"

Oh, my goodness! We all laughed, "Yeah, that would be worse!"

Resigned to the fact that we had to stay home, the kids went on the cruise and chatted with us by email every day. We heard all about the scrumptious scones, fresh pizza, and the beautiful sights in Italy. We felt like we were on the trip with them. Steph kept reassuring me how difficult the trip would have been for her dad, and how exhausted they actually were themselves. There was so much walking, and they assured me that I never could have pushed him in a wheelchair over cobblestones! Somehow that did help us accept the fact that staying home was the better option for us, and we soon enjoyed a truly happy reunion, beautiful gifts from Italy, and all their wonderful stories.

By October 2012, five months into Daryle's treatment, we had adjusted to a new routine. After so many victories, the seizures signaled a turn for the worse and ushered in a season of disappointments. Every new upset forced a new "normal" on us. We had been so hopeful, but now learned that anaplastic astrocytoma (tumor, the kind Daryle had), "play dead." They go underground and come back with greater fury. The tumor looked like an octopus, and its tentacles now reached new territory, meaning more medications, incontinence, and a slew of other problems as the cancer attacked new centers in the brain. I recall praying and promising the Lord that I would take care of Daryle forever if only He would allow it. I would accept as many "new normals" as He decreed. I loved Daryle and was willing to do anything God asked of me.

I constantly updated our son Rick about all the changes in his dad's condition. He would come down as often as possible to spend time with Daryle, and during every visit they watched *IP Man* together (a martial arts movie), imitating karate chops and eating popcorn. The funny thing is that they watched that movie together a hundred times because Daryle never remembered from one visit to the next that they had just watched it on Rick's previous visit. But this part of our routine took me back to a sweeter time when they regularly played video games together, watched movies, and joked around. Seeing Rick hanging out with his dad brought me comfort and at the same time created a false feeling of normalcy.

Unfortunately, things weren't normal. Up to this point I'd been perfectly healthy, but caring for Daryle was a physical challenge for me. Lifting his 6'2," 230 lb. frame with my 5'5" 130 lb. body was tough. The strain began to manifest in me with severe throbbing in my left leg. I kept trying to ignore it because I was so consumed with Daryle's care, but the excruciating pain was making it impossible to walk with him or help him in the shower, or get him dressed. I was getting extremely frustrated and was eventually forced to care for myself.

I finally told Daryle about it and he said, "Love, next time we go to see the vascular doctor, tell him about it." Why didn't I think of that? I did, and his doctor and I decided on a procedure to alleviate my pain. I had the hardest time convincing Daryle that it would be better for him to wait at home rather than to come with me. He desperately wanted to be there for me, as I had been for him, but I was more concerned that while I was having surgery, he might have a seizure and fall in the waiting room. Or worse, that he wouldn't fully understand that the doctors were trying to help me.

He reluctantly agreed to stay home. I promised to call during the actual procedure to reassure him that I was okay. It only took an hour, and when they finished, they wrapped my leg from hip to toe and I headed home. When I walked through the door, Daryle was so upset to see me bound in bandages, his mouth dropped open. "My lady, look at you. What did they do to you?" He was distressed but so excited to be able to take care of me for a change, as he happily shuffled into the kitchen to make me tea and toast.

During my first evening recuperating at home, we went to bed in our converted sitting room downstairs and settled in for the night. Around 1:30 a.m., Daryle shook my shoulder.

"Yes, honey. What is it?"

"I'm having trouble breathing."

"Oh, boy. OK. That's too much for me. I'm calling 911."

They kept me on the landline until the ambulance got there, and while I waited, I called my parents on my cell phone. They quickly got dressed and came over. Pastor John also came to help in any way possible. My heart was racing, and the feeling of complete and utter helplessness filled my soul. We were approximately four months into Daryle's cancer: what could this possibly be now? I went to the hospital with him, and they quickly determined that many large blood clots had shot from his legs to his lungs.

Now as far as blood clots go, one half the size of your pinky fingernail can kill you, and only 3 percent of patients survive the type Daryle had. Daryle's doctors came in, shook his hand, and said they didn't know how he was alive because the x-ray revealed a saddle pulmonary embolism, which apparently can lead very rapidly to death. Saddle pulmonary embolisms literally fill the lungs and block the blood flow to the lungs, making the person highly unstable. I saw the X-rays! If the embolus moves, it can completely cut off the supply of blood, leading to sudden death. I said, "I will tell you how he is alive. It's by the grace of God that he sits before you. He is a miracle!"

"Yes, he is," replied the doctors. Daryle should have died. But God had other plans.

Now I began ten days of back and forth to the hospital. Daryle received more meds, including warfarin, and more procedures, including INR (international normalized ratio). Daily INR checks watched how his blood coagulated. Regulating his INR was a nightmare that was about to become a constant in our lives. Everything that Daryle ate effected his coagulation. If he ate too few leafy greens, his blood would become too thin, and he would run the risk of hemorrhaging. It was a constant balancing act. All the while they poked and prodded him. Daryle was tired and annoyed with the hourly blood draws to check his levels. He looked like a multicolored (bruised) pincushion. The doctors informed us that it would take months and months for the blood clots to be reabsorbed into his body. Daryle just wanted to go home. I just reassured him that everyone at church was praying for a speedy recovery, and for God to do something miraculous.

My sister Tra happened to be at the church and texted this statement from a friend who believed she had heard from the Lord during the service. "I have heard your prayers. Now watch Me move."

What? Oh, my goodness. How exciting! I showed Daryle and an hour later we received our answer.

The doctor came in. His name was Dr. Stahpit (pronounced "Stop it" … you couldn't make this up). He proceeded to tell us that the latest x-ray, taken an hour before, revealed that the blood clots in his lungs had disappeared!

I asked, "What do you mean 'disappeared'? Where did they go? I thought you said it would take months and months."

"Yes—well, they are gone."

The first question was, "Can we go home?" Before the ink on the release papers dried, Daryle was dressed and ready. We left and called the church to report the miraculous news. I can tell you there was a lot of hooting and hollering going on! Praise God! Praise God! I just knew this was it … the beginning of the completion of his healing. We were absolutely convinced!

Stephanie would spend as much time as she could with her dad now that he was settled back home, and Rick called as often as possible. They always looked on the bright side, especially as Daryle seemed to be getting stronger again. What a gift this was to me as (drumroll) I was about to turn fifty! It's always a little crazy around my birthday, because it's in November at the beginning of the holiday season. I had been out shopping with my mom and returned to find that our daughter Stephanie and our niece Taylor had decorated our home with a ton of twinkle lights. They'd set the table in the shabby chic style that I love, using 100-year-old china with a bouquet of gorgeous pink roses in the center. Beautiful handmade ornaments were placed all around the crocheted antique tablecloth. My nephew, a professional chef, made one of my favorite gourmet fish dishes. Oh, my goodness. It was just the most beautiful night. All the people I love, and of course my hubby, were with me. It was a dream. I noticed my husband had on dress clothes and I asked him, "Who helped you get dressed?"

He replied with pride, "I dressed myself!" It must have taken him an hour because at this stage, this was no easy task. His feat was icing on the cake and I didn't want the night to end.

Soon the holidays were upon us. Daryle's progress was so uplifting that Thanksgiving was a blast. We all wore the "turkey hat," a Borrows tradition, and told silly stories about how we'd acted like "turkeys" over the past year, or any other time. Daryle even wore the turkey hat and, standing there leaning on his cane, told a hilarious story from his youth that he clearly remembered. We all knew the story but didn't let on because we were so thrilled and thankful to God that Daryle could recall every last detail. It was pure joy to see him so alive and engaged and animated.

Before we knew it, Christmas Day arrived! We loved Christmas, and this year we were especially grateful to God for the gift of Daryle's miraculous deliverance from the deadly embolism. Daryle shuffled his feet over to our stockings, sat down and read his traditional Christmas morning scripture to us, Luke chapter 2. We had a great day with the family and opened gifts in shifts all the daylong. It was the best celebration. Snapping a few photos, I thought, "What if this is his last Christmas? NO! I refuse to go there! This is going to be a great new year!"

CHAPTER 6

WINTER

On December 30th, 2012, Stephanie and her husband, Kevin, came by the house. As Steph walked into our kitchen, she told me, "Oh Mom, I have something for you!" She handed it to me and I suddenly realized that it was an EPT test. POSITIVE! They were going to have a baby! Our hearts were overwhelmed. We were jumping and shouting for joy. She was due in September, which was so neat because her birthday was in September.

"Steph, you are going to be pregnant during the same months that I was," I told her.

Steph asked her dad, "Hey Dad, what do you want the baby to call you?"

"I like Grandpa."

"Okay, great."

A few months later, Steph wondered if he remembered what he had said, and she repeated the question.

A little annoyed, he responded, "I already told you, Nef (Steph's nickname). Grandpa! I haven't forgotten everything, you know." We laughed, happy to see a little feistiness in him. This was a good sign.

Now came the planning. What fun. Something great was coming. Daryle always wanted to be a grandpa. Back when our babies were little, he would speak of them having babies and us taking them all to Disneyworld. Of course, my response was, "Well, can we let our own kids grow up first, honey?"

January was a very routine month. All was well. We had three birthdays to celebrate and the birthday parties were held at our house. Daryle walked with a cane to keep his balance. It seemed to really help him. He was a great patient and never really complained about anything. I often told him that I didn't think I would be as good a patient as he was. I'm a "let's get going" person, and he enjoyed just laying back. Funny how we could be so different in some ways, but we were so compatible.

February was crazy! For some nutty reason, our basic appliances were revolting. The washing machine was banging, our car was banging, and it just seemed to be everything at once. We live in Westport, Massachusetts, and February 7–9th brought its own challenges. Nemo, a monster Nor'easter, was a beast of a storm that dumped 27 inches of snow on us. My biggest concern of course was losing power. I had to keep Daryle warm. The warfarin thinned his blood, leaving him so cold that his fingers turned blue. Under normal circumstances, I had to take extreme measures to keep him warm: keeping the thermostat in the seventies, covering him with extra blankets in addition to the down comforter, etc. If we lost heat now, I didn't know what other measures I would have been able to take.

Thankfully he was determined that we get a generator, so we went shopping and brought one home. Even in his condition, he was obsessed with making sure it worked. I said, "Babe, it's fine. It will work. Please don't worry yourself." I made sure we had everything we needed, including extra medication, and when the storm hit, we did lose power for three days! That generator saved us. It kept Daryle warm and both of us safe. It was Daryle's idea and he was pleased as punch.

I remember praying about the storm and asking God how in the world I was going to dig us out all by myself, and the scripture "that happened to appear" in my devotional for that day was "And you shall be secure, because there is hope, yes, you shall dig about you, and you shall take your rest in safety." (Job 11:18, AKJV) I came in from shoveling and Daryle was in quite a state! I asked him, "What's the matter, honey?"

"Well, it's not right that everyone is out there shoveling while I'm stuck in here."

"Well, love, you could fall. It's really slippery," I said in my concerned tone.

"I don't care. I want to help."

"Okay," I said hesitantly because I didn't want him to go out, but I dressed him in multiple layers, put on his boots, and we ventured outdoors.

It took three of us to get him down the stairs. I handed him a shovel and he started going at it. Shuffling and shoveling, he was the cutest thing ever! The family was eyeballing him the whole time, and he made his way over to our car when it happened ... his feet flew out from under him, and the shovel went flying! We all rushed to him and honestly it was like a comedy act. We were trying to get him up and we were all falling. It's hard to be serious when you are laughing! It did take a while, but once we all got back inside, he stated, "If I ever forget, remind me that I don't want to do that again!"

"Okay, love. Deal!"

Time was passing. I kept trying to remember life before brain cancer. Memories flooded my mind, especially those of him with the kids when they were young. Rick remembers his dad enthusiastically waking him up early in the morning to go to catch the waking fish. I remembered the days when Stephanie wore his shoes and told him that they were her shoes. I remembered them playing airplane, board games, cards, enjoying movie nights, and homemade popcorn. Oh, how he loved his children. What special memories we'd made. I recalled our own date nights and our many "let's just go for a drive" adventures. I wanted the days back that I was losing; the days when I waited for him to come home because I missed him so, and when we headed out to a movie just to hold hands in the dark. It was all wonderful. Daryle would get upset with me if I did not call him every day on his way to work, even though we'd just said goodbye. I'd say, "Honey, I live with you. You see me every day." But he always answered, "You don't understand, love. Yours is the best voice I hear every day. My Cheese, I love you!"

I remembered one of the best compliments Daryle ever gave me. One day I saw his head bob by the window as he climbed the steps to our home. I ran to open the door to meet him and gave him a big hug. He said, "Honey, I stink from working all day."

I replied, "I don't care. Give me a kiss!"

He replied, "I love coming home to you."

He would take hold of my hand and sing a line from a song that he enjoyed that basically said we just walk along on a summer's day, nothing to do, nothing to say, just walking with my love another day.

That was once upon a time, but now I felt like he was slipping away from me and, no matter how hard I tried, I couldn't bring him back.

More recent memories were not so welcome. I recalled when we had asked the doctor how long the tumor had been in Daryle's brain. The doctor told us that it usually takes about two years to present itself. What a revelation! That means it began in May of 2010 when God woke Daryle to give him the scriptures, including "Number 4," the tumor was already growing in his brain. Now it all made sense. God gave Daryle a heads up back then that something was coming.

There was another memory from when we first married over thirty years before that was downright extraordinary considering our present circumstances. My husband once asked me, "Honey, if I got sick someday, what would you do?"

I said without hesitation, "I would take care of you."

A great big smile came over his face and he seemed relieved. I wondered why he would ask such a bizarre question. I asked, "Did you think I wouldn't?"

He answered, "No, I thought that's what you'd say, but it is reassuring to hear it. It's just that in some war movies, wives would leave their wedding rings on the bedside table and just walk out on their husbands when they were sick, and the thought goes through your mind."

I sternly replied, "Well, they obviously did not love their husbands like I love you. You are my Cheese 'til death do us part, which isn't going to happen! Oh, and PS: no more war movies for you!"

You know, you say, "'til death do us part" on your wedding day, but you never really think it will happen to you until you're old and gray. It seems kind of crazy because we hear it all the time. This person died, that person died, but surely, not US! Well, why not us? The Bible says, "For he gives his sunlight to both the evil and the good, and he sends rain on the just and the unjust alike." (Matthew 5:45, NLT) I understood this in my spirit but even so, my soul was in anguish. It was just so dark, lonely, and cold. I felt like I could barely catch my breath as waves battered against me, and as I was trying to save myself, I was trying to save Daryle too. Constantly trying to rise above our reality was the hardest thing I'd ever done. Our daily habit became declaring God's truth and remembering the heroes of faith in God's word. "Abraham acted in faith when he stood in the presence of God, who gives life to the dead and calls into existence things that don't yet exist." (Romans 4:17, ISV) That's what we were doing ... speaking God's Word in faith over Daryle, but our words of faith were often at odds with what our eyes could see. That was our dilemma.

The healing that we continued to pray for was slow in coming. We were hopeful and steadfast in prayer and faith, but life day to day was hard. Despite the miracles and little victories, Daryle knew he was declining, and he knew what it was doing to me. Humor still helped. And God used the oddest things to make us laugh. My laundry had grown to gigantic proportions. I decided to bleach out all of Daryle's whites, his t-shirts, underwear, and socks. How a random piece of red fabric finds its way into a white wash I will never know! Needless to say, everything came out pink! Well, I didn't have time to rewash the whole load, so I thought, "Here's hoping he doesn't notice."

You know he may have had a brain tumor, but there was nothing wrong with those baby blues! "Uh, honey, why are my socks pink, and my t-shirt and hey, my underwear?"

"Babe, I'm so sorry, but I didn't have time to rewash them. Besides, it's just us. No one will see them."

"Okay, but there's just something unmanly about this."

Well, later that day he experienced new pain in his neck, and I had to take him to the emergency room. No kidding. Daryle laughed out loud, "Oh? Nobody is going to see my pink socks, pink t-shirt, or pink underwear?"

I giggled, "Honey! How could I have known we would end up here today?"

My best friend Michelle showed up and Daryle said, "Michelle, look what she did to me!" Funny memories ... I thank God for them. We had a few hilarious chuckles along our crazy journey.

It was now Valentine's Day 2013 and our thirty-second wedding anniversary. Daryle asked our daughter to shop for him, and he surprised me with beautiful red roses and a gift. I ordered his favorite food from Olive Garden. We had a nice dinner together laughing and talking. I know God's word tells us to "take captive every thought to make it obedient to Christ." (2 Corinthians 10:5, NIV) I was trying desperately to do that, but the negative idea that this would be our last Valentine's Day together kept pushing in. It was a wonderful day and I focused on the sweet memories of our life together that danced in my head.

I reminisced about when I first met Daryle back in 1973. We were both very young. I was eleven and he was fourteen. We had very different lives. He grew up in a loving Christian home surrounded by church folks. We rarely went to church and my home life was troubled. My parents met in Germany and I was born in Northern Ireland. My dad, Paul, was in the army and my Irish mom, Jessie, was on holiday with her friends when they met. They fell in love and soon married. The catch was that he lived in the United States. My parents started a family in Europe. But with me in tow, my mom and dad eventually made the move to Massachusetts. Now separated from her own home and extended family in Ireland, our family grew within a year and a half to include my sister and my brother a full eight years later. We witnessed a lot as kids including the disintegration of their marriage and the auctioning of our childhood home.

Despite the differences in our upbringing, God was going to knit our lives together and unify our families. When my mom had had enough, she divorced the man she had once loved. My mom became a citizen of this country and put herself through nursing school, but something was lacking in her life. Then a divine connection was made. My mom met Lil Borrows (Daryle's mom) at the nursing home where they both worked. Lil convinced her to come to her church, and she agreed. We, on the other hand, were against it.

"Church! Why?" we whined. "Don't argue. We are going!" Ugh! My sister Tra and I walked through the door and an older gentleman said, "Welcome, boys!" Boys! Highly insulted, we shouted, "We are not boys! What kind of place is this, Mom?" I guess at ten and eleven it was hard to tell we were girls, if you get my meaning.

Anyway, there he was, Daryle Wayne, standing in his navy blue polyester double-breasted suit! He had a badge on that stated he was an usher. We said hello and he asked if he could show us a seat. "No," I said. "I'm quite capable of finding my own seat!"

"Well, fine. Sit where you want." Ah, young love. He told me later that when he first saw me, the word "marriage" came into his mind.

I told him, "Good thing you never mentioned that to me!" I didn't have a high view of marriage. My dad was not chivalrous or very kind to me. I took it as an insult if Daryle opened a door for me. I really had never been exposed to gentlemanly behavior and wondered if he had had an ulterior motive.

We attended church for just a few weeks before we all gave our lives to Jesus. We said, "If You are real, God, we need You." And from that moment on, we jumped tracks and our lives were in sync with God's plan. The lightbulb went on. We experienced a strange connection that we had no words for... a personal warmth came over all of us, that I know now was the Presence of God. We didn't want to leave this comforting presence. Afterwards, people I knew outside of church noticed a visible change in my countenance and asked, "What's wrong with you?" I told them that I'd accepted Jesus, like the preacher said, and that something happened to me. I tried to explain that it was as if there was a golden rope permanently between Heaven and me. My perception of reality was suddenly so much bigger. The desire for the Lord overwhelmed me. At the age of eleven I wanted more. I'd never known the pure, deep love of a father, but God became my real Father and His church became our extended family.

My mom and Lil were very close and, as it turns out, they began plotting our future almost immediately! One day my mom let me in on the fact that she and Lil were praying that we would get together and I replied, "Well, I'm praying that God doesn't listen to your prayer!"

Daryle and I started dating mostly because I was trying to get people off my back. I came up with this grand plan that I would date him for two weeks and then I could say I tried. Then I would break up with him and all would be well. I came home and bellowed, "Mom, are you home? Guess who I am dating?" Elated, she immediately called Lil and they were both giddy. I could hear my mom saying, "He did what?" I wondered what in the world was going on. Mom hung up the phone and shared what Lil had said. Daryle had run hooting and hollering up the stairs, shouting, "She said yes! She said yes!" Seriously, why? I was fourteen. He was seventeen and about to graduate high school. This was nuts!

We went to the movies, laughed a lot, and had many dates in those two weeks. Despite my annoyance, he continued to open doors for me and to show me great kindness. He bought me a coffee mug that was engraved, "How long will I love you? Only always." Oh, boy. My two weeks were suddenly up. I had to rethink my plan as my icy heart had softened to the point of melting. I fell head over heels for him and he for me. I guess the moms were right! And God heard their prayers. Yay for moms!

We dated for a couple of years and when I turned sixteen, he asked me to marry him. We'd known each other for years and knew that we were bound to each other. This wasn't puppy love. We knew most outsiders would think this was totally inappropriate, but we didn't care. My high school English teacher tried unsuccessfully to get me to postpone the wedding, citing with genuine concern that we didn't really know what we were getting into. He made a $10 bet with me that it wouldn't last ten years. We renewed our wedding vows on our tenth anniversary, and I made him publicly pay me $10. He said he was never so happy to be wrong, and on our twentieth he sent us a card with $20 in it!

We got married on Valentine's Day 1981. I was eighteen but still in high school. We went to Disneyworld for our honeymoon. It was so great because we were really just big kids who were madly in love. We settled into married life while I was still in school. I was in a program where I took my major classes for half the day then went to work the other half. Now that I was a married woman, I was allowed to write my own absentee notes when I wasn't in school (which was fun). Our days and weeks passed happily as we waited three years to start our own family. We were blessed as our families lived, loved, and worked together, dedicating the next thirty years of our lives to our church and congregation. I was even my father-in-law's secretary for nineteen years. We hoped we were doing good together and saw many people give their hearts to the Lord.

I loved my walks down memory lane. They were a temporary escape from facing an increasingly hard reality. So here we were Valentine's Day 2013; I kept reminding myself over and over that the Bible promises that all things work together for good for those who love the Lord and are called according to His purpose. But my question continued to be, "How can this ever be good and what is the purpose?" Fighting the doldrums was the smallest of our problems. I would plan an outing, even if just to go shopping. But I had to laugh as I wrestled with his wheelchair, wondering if anyone else knew how heavy that monster was. I pushed Daryle around but at first he bucked me thinking this was an outing for an old man, but God even blessed in this. We transitioned to a motorized cart, and then Daryle was all set because he could do it himself. Once again, we made fun out of the silliest situations. I would pile things up on Daryle and Steph and I would tease him by sending him in the wrong direction. When he finally realized we were messing with him, he'd spin around and chase us down. Man, I loved that guy.

CHAPTER 7

SPRING

Spring 2013 was a new season, one that heralds the promise of new life and new opportunity. We loved road trips but hadn't been able to leave town for months and were so excited to receive my brother's invitation to his retirement from the Air Force in South Carolina. Paul hoped that Mom, Randy, Daryle, and I could join him to celebrate his achievement. Daryle was ecstatic and wanted to go the minute we got the news. He was so proud of my brother, whom he'd known since Paul was three. He didn't want to miss the chance to congratulate him in person. Daryle could not fly, so we wondered if we could drive. Would he be okay to go the distance approximately 900 miles away?

My parents got the minivan ready and we were off to the races. We hit a lot of rest stops along the way but he did well, and we were all encouraged. We laughed, talked, told stories, and had a very enjoyable trip. We got to Sumter, South Carolina, and my brother Paul, his wife Christina, and their daughters Jordin and Jackie, all came running out to greet us. They had graciously invited us all to stay in their home which was just a five-minute walk from a little pond surrounded by pine straw where Paul and I loved to go fishing.

Soon after our arrival we decided to do just that. I asked Daryle, "Are you sure you're okay if I leave you with everyone and go fishing with Paul?"

"Go, honey. Have fun with your brother. I'm fine. Don't worry." I felt such relief. I loved Daryle beyond belief, but I was so grateful just for a little "away" time. Knowing that Daryle was safe in the care of my family and that I could enjoy time alone with my only brother, I immediately felt my batteries begin to refresh and recharge. I had been on my guard 24/7 and believed that if I let my guard down for a second, something awful would happen. Until this moment, I had not realized how desperately I needed a reprieve. I needed a moment to be more than a caretaker or nurse or wife. Paul made me feel like a kid again. No matter how long we'd been apart, whenever Paul and I got back together, it was like old times. We are very close, but we also bring out the funny in each other. They say laughter is good medicine and my time with Paul was medicine for me.

We were having a blast talking about old times, catching little fishes, but still going after the big one! We had only been there about 15 minutes when Daryle called my cell phone. "Honey, when are you coming back? You've been gone for hours."

"Umm, babe. It's only been 15 minutes, but I will come now."

Shocked, he replied, "What! No way! OK, love. Don't come now. You have a good time. Keep on fishing."

"Are you sure?"

"Yep." My brother couldn't believe it. "Wow, Q" (short for Suzie Q), "you are really going through it."

"Yeah, but he's worth it." Two minutes later, the phone rang again.

It was the same story. "I'm on my way, my love." It must have been awful for Daryle thinking that I'd deserted him for hours. I came to the realization that I just couldn't leave him anymore. He just didn't understand.

During our visit, nighttime was difficult too. I was always on alert due to his frequent need to use the bathroom. I did not get much sleep. It was happening more and more in the daytime as well. The need for supervision was constant. He was trying to walk with the cane and was propping himself against the wall, sliding his way down the hall in an effort to be independent. As I walked alongside him, I prayed, "Lord, what am I missing? How can I help him? He is so frustrated."

God answered. A thought came to mind about using a walker. So, while he napped, I left him with the family and darted to Walmart. I found the perfect walker for him. It looked fabulous once I assembled it. It had a seat with a little hidden storage basket for when he needed a rest. It even had brakes. It was quite the little buggy. He loved it, and we nicknamed him Speedy Gonzalez because he pushed that thing speedily all over the house. It was like a new toy at Christmas. He kept anything he needed in the seat: his music, his water, his phone. Now that he had "wheels," he asked, "My lady, would you like to go for a walk with me?" How sweet! It truly was a Godsend.

My brother's retirement ceremony was terrific. Daryle was determined to walk in under his own power, so he left the walker behind and made his way into the building just using the cane. My man still had pride and wanted to stand up in the presence of all these heroes. They shook his hand and said, "You keep fighting, sir!" Daryle got to speak with some military higher-ups and he was thrilled, being the military history buff that he was. It was an absolute highlight for him.

The next morning Paul and Randy took Daryle for breakfast and a haircut on Shaw Air Force Base. They stopped at the "BX" (military mall) fishing store and my beloved saw a fishing pole that he thought I would like. As they were checking out, Daryle asked the woman if she knew his pin number, "I just can't remember it." Crazy enough the pin was "bass," a fish. Confused, she said, "No, sir. I do not." Paul stepped in and said, "Do it as credit, no pin needed." The guys relayed this story to me upon their return. I thought, "What is happening here? Is he getting worse?" I thought he looked good. Yet my brother mentioned that the girls were shocked to see how much he had deteriorated. Though there may have been decline in his body and in his brain, we decided to play a "brain game" called "Things." What was really funny was that Daryle beat us all! He said, "Hey, I'm the one with brain cancer. You should all know this stuff!" We all enjoyed quite a few laughs over that.

The next day was tough. To my brother, this farewell felt like it would be the last. The journey home was much more difficult than the trip down. Many more stops were needed, and when we finally made it to our hotel at midnight, we were all hoping to rest. Unfortunately, there was some kind of party on the floor above us and we had to call repeatedly to make them stop. Daryle was highly agitated and uneasy. The next morning, we got our breakfast and headed off again. Randy was driving and Daryle was in the front seat insisting that Randy keep driving by the same place over and over. He would mention, "Honey, I saw that gas station before." His brain was having a hard time adjusting to the traveling and seeing his rapidly changing surroundings. I had to ask him if he could see that we were moving forward, but he was sure we had been driving around in circles. The brain is a marvelous and mysterious thing.

We made it home and I think Daryle slept for about 20 hours! Our first day home, our daughter came to visit. Her pregnancy was coming along, and Daryle would joyfully pat her belly and say hello to the baby. The day came when we were to find out the sex of the baby. We were so excited! My niece Taylor videoed the whole "reveal." We sat together as Steph and Kevin came in holding a gift bag. We reached in knowing that the color of the outfit would tell us the result.

Hooray. It was a girl! Madison … Madelyn … not sure of the baby's name, but we were thrilled. Steph asked me if I would go in with her and Kevin for the birth. I was ecstatic. I had something wonderful to look forward to.

A few days later, I was on the phone with Daryle's nurse from Dana Farber. I was looking at him but turned my back for a split second and BOOM! I spun around and he was on the floor. I ran over, crouched down next to him, and said, "Are you okay? Does anything hurt?"

"I'm fine, honey. I was trying to grab the remote and lost my balance." The nurse asked me to bring him in right away to do another MRI. "Right away" meant an hour-and-a-half trip to Boston without traffic. That test confirmed that the cancer had spread to his spine. There was nothing we could do.

"Jesus! No! No! We are having a grandbaby. This cannot be the truth. This is a lie! God, come through for him!" I was crying uncontrollably.

We left there utterly discouraged. The pressure on my chest was so crushing, I literally felt like my ribs would crack from the stress. I cried to Daryle, "Please, don't leave me. I love you beyond words. I can't live this life without you."

"Honey, I'm not going anywhere. Doctors are not always right." We lived by faith and actively chose to walk by faith, not by sight. We understood that what is extreme faith to the believer is denial to the unbeliever. People actually said that to me. I knew that until God's final decree was clear, we were to trust and hope in Him. Until HE reveals our final day, our final hour, our final breath, we are to expect miracles from Him because that is the God we serve.

Even if Daryle believed what they said, and even if he knew that he was fading, he always tried to comfort me. He was more concerned for me than he was for himself. Our church family kicked it into high gear at this point, and our friends stopped by and put a prayer shawl around our shoulders as they prayed a beautiful, powerful prayer over us. It was very encouraging. Our whole family and many friends stood in solidarity with us and marched around our house seven times, like Joshua around the walls of Jericho, praying for a victorious outcome! Despite so many standing in the gap and so much support, I often found myself struggling inconsolably. My poor family! They went through all the anguish with me and for me.

My sister Tra did everything she could to be an encouragement to us. Tra has had her own share of suffering dealing with rheumatoid arthritis most of her life. I had always been there for her during dozens of surgeries and I watched as she faithfully pressed on. She always encouraged others to trust and believe that God could do mighty things. Now she was there for me, comforting me in my growing darkness. Tra is an artist. She painted a picture to capture the feelings I described to her. She painted the blackest of black rooms, with swirls of light penetrating through as the dark tried to extinguish them. She also encouraged Daryle to write a song, which he did. He picked up his guitar and with his hat on and blanket around his shoulders, he plucked away, and sang a song that he named "He Sustains." These are the words to his very last song, "God holds the future in His hands, even when we don't understand. Though it's hard to let go, His will we know. It will all work out in the end."

This experience felt more and more like a freight train barreling towards us while we stood immobilized, unable to get off the deadly tracks! Life was progressing, but not in the direction we had prayed for. Everything had become an enormous ongoing problem every hour of every day. Daryle could no longer hold and drink from a cup without spilling the contents all over himself. He couldn't use a straw because he might choke, so I now had to teach him how to drink from a special medical Provale cup which only poured one teaspoon of liquid per tilt. He kept forgetting how to use it and I repeatedly had to explain. This was incredibly tedious for Daryle and for me, but it was a lifesaver. Daryle could no longer get out of bed, so it was now necessary for me to order a hospital bed for the living room. I also needed a Hoyer (a hydraulic lift) to move him from the bed to the chair. Caring for Daryle was a massive undertaking: from the minutest daily activity to all of Daryle's medical conditions to every basic physical need. My teenage experience as a CNA (certified nursing assistant) in nursing homes definitely helped me with the practical challenges I now faced, but I struggled constantly with the emotional challenge.

The definition of "despair" is "the loss of hope, hopelessness." I don't think this adequately describes what I felt and what he felt. We would gaze into each other's eyes and tears would drip down our cheeks, communicating a lifetime of love without words. I don't want to give the illusion that we were perfect people or a perfect couple. We went the rounds like everyone does, but what we did know through it all was "Only Always." Our love was forever. Daryle let me be me. Many times he would come home from work to find that the furniture was moved around, or a wall had been demolished (I was the original

HGTV girl). He would just exclaim, "It's a good thing I'm not blind!" Nine times out of ten he liked what I had changed, even though he himself would have never ever changed anything! He would say, "All I need is a bed, couch, TV, fridge, and a clock." To me that seemed boring! How different we were!

People started to come more and more to see him. I called one set of visitors in particular, "Job's three friends" (found in the Old Testament Book of Job). In their own way they thought they were doing good, but they'd never come to our home before or offered any kind of support or assistance. On one unfortunate day, they came to the house to give us advice to make sure we weren't "doing it wrong."

They first wanted to make sure that Daryle wasn't hindering his healing by holding any grudges or unforgiveness toward others. Then, noticing that I helped Daryle with his drink, they offered their advice that I should let him do it himself. My sister could see the mother bear in me rising up and put her hand gently on my arm to persuade me not to rip their heads off. I kindly pulled them aside and let them know in no uncertain terms that they had no idea what we were going through on a daily basis, and if they thought this was helpful, they were wrong. Their actions felt more insulting than anything. More pain and judgment was certainly not what we needed. I said, "Thanks, but no thanks. It's time for you to leave. My husband has made peace with his maker and any who hurt him through the years. He himself made sure he apologized to anyone whom he may have hurt." How I admired my beautiful man. Watching me as I ushered "Job's friends" to the front door, he said, "Look at my woman go!"

I was so grateful that most who visited us during this trying time were a blessing. We received a phone call that Darlene and Daryle's brother Todd were coming. What welcome company they would be! I tried to prepare her for the reality that Daryle was not as spry as when she last saw him; in fact, he was often bedridden. It was a wonderful time for us all to be together. Mum happily helped us both while she was there and she could see for herself that he wasn't doing well. She knew firsthand what he was going through. When Darlene was younger, she had ovarian cancer and almost lost her life. Praise God she made it through. She was now hoping and praying the same for him.

Their visit was good for Daryle. Todd is a jokester, and he had Daryle laughing constantly. He is a very positive person and my love needed that. Todd is also a survivor who had had his own trauma a few years before. While driving in the mountains of Colorado, a rock rolled down the mountain and smashed into his windshield, crushing half of his skull. After so many years of surgeries and seizures he could relate to Daryle, and spoke knowingly and compassionately to Daryle about what he was actually going through. He knew all about it firsthand. What are the odds that two brothers would both experience brain trauma? They shared a special bond that was precious.

As Darlene and Todd got ready to return home, we faced another hard good-bye. I wondered if this was going to be the last time Darlene would see her son alive. My heart ached for her, realizing that she had already said good-bye to Daryle as a baby. After being apart from him for so many years, this might be her final goodbye. I kept her informed as to how he was doing in the days that followed.

Daryle and I felt the heaviness of their parting and thought a mindless distraction might be nice, so we decided to watch the Boston Marathon. Sadly, this day in April of 2013, Boston became the site of a terrorist act that brought heartache, tragedy, and loss of life. We grieved because we had just been on Boylston Street in Boston with

Darlene the day before for an appointment at Dana Farber. We personally understood the struggle and the anguish of those who suffered that terrible day.

It also became personal for us because in the next few days, our neighborhood in Westport, Massachusetts, was crawling with police. We live five minutes from UMass Dartmouth where one of the bombers was a registered student. Our neighborhood was on high alert because the bombers had disappeared, and the authorities were on a massive manhunt through our community. We were watching it on TV as we heard them blaze down our street. Though we had all been told to stay in our homes, I had to drive by the college to run to the store to get Daryle's medications. The police presence was unprecedented.

When I got back home, Daryle mentioned that Martin William Richard, the little boy who died, looked just like our boy when he was little. Our son's name is Richard William Borrows. This was too much for Daryle. His brain was short-circuiting on adrenalin and fear. He was confused and kept asking me if that was our Ricky. He insisted that I get up repeatedly to check the locks to make sure the "bad guys" couldn't get in. We had to turn the news off and I tried to lighten the moment, saying, "Back to the Home and Garden Channel it is!"

Daryle used to tease me calling it the "Home and Garbage Channel." One day I came back home from work to find him watching it!

"Really?"

Daryle's reply: "*Love It or List It*… it's not that bad."

I was definitely an HGTV wannabe! Our home had a tub in the bathroom. I'd begun to have trouble getting Daryle's leg over the tub. I decided, "That's it. I'm installing a walk-in shower!" In the midst of managing all the medical equipment and healthcare procedures, I started a DIY project with demolition, construction, tiles, plaster dust, and drywall. In hindsight, I was not being rational. I was driven by the thought that if I could help Daryle in any way, I would, and if Daryle needed something, I was determined to get it. So if Daryle needed a shower, he was getting a shower.

I quickly realized I was in over my head and couldn't possibly care for my husband *and* build a new bathroom, so I enlisted our friend Tom to "help" me. In fact, Tom rescued me. I would take pictures of the progress and show Daryle. He loved it and seemed really engaged at first, but I sensed something was changing. Daryle seemed to be going downhill quickly.

As Daryle deteriorated, so did many of the comments of his well-meaning visitors.

"We just hope he makes it till the baby is born."

"If he dies, it's God's will."

"Will you move away if he dies?"

Are you kidding me? Everyone leave me alone! His face was thinning, and he seemed to have a grayish tone. What hadn't changed was his sense of humor. He was lying in the bed because he no longer had the strength to get to the bathroom, and my mom was helping me as I washed him. Mom would roll him as I tended to him, and Daryle kept saying, "Ouch, ouch, ouch!"

I responded, "I'm so sorry. I'm sorry, honey. Sorry"

He jokingly teased, "There's an awful lot of sorry going on!"

We laughed and thought that deserved a kiss. Smooch smooch!

I was so grateful for Daryle's love and his continued presence in my life, but his acute pain and growing weakness heightened the tug of war between my faith and my reality. One second I felt like I'm winning this bad boy, and the next I'm in the mud. I wondered if there's a "better" way, a less agonizing way, to lose the one you love. I know many women lose their husbands instantly and tragically, but here I was wondering for almost a full year, "Is this the day? Is it today?"

Another day he told me, "I feel like I'm soaring."

"You listen to me," I said, "There will be no soaring! Don't you even think about it! It will NOT be today. Do you hear me?"

A half smiling smirk came over him and more smooches followed. But this one statement set me shaking uncontrollably to the point that I could not steady my own hands from that day forward. Something went "click" and I thought "OK. Here we go. Oh, God. He's leaving me. I see it. I know it. I can't stop it. And I can't stop this trembling. Maybe I will die of it? NO, he needs me, and I need him. I can do all things through Christ who gives me strength. Please give me strength for all things, Jesus." I was weary. I was shaking, but I was still believing 100 percent for a miracle. I didn't care what my eyes showed me, my faith sight was stronger than my vision, and I believed God could resurrect from death, even if death should come.

CHAPTER 8

FINAL DAZE

I could see he was slipping away. Hospice came back and presented me with the DNR papers again. The nurse was so kind, and my mom held me. They explained that if I did not sign the papers and he died, they would break his ribs to bring him back. As my knees literally knocked together, I dry-heaved and quivered from head to toe. I signed the DNR. I knew that as Daryle lay in the living room no more than ten feet from me, he could hear us and knew what we were doing. He had been asked to do the same for his own father. I felt like I was signing his death warrant. I knew I was going to be sick and ran to the bathroom. As I turned green, Daryle began to aspirate. I was gagging. Suctioning his throat is the one thing I could not do. I thanked God that my mom was a respiratory nurse! I huddled in a fetal position on the bed in the other room and blocked my ears so that I would not hear my beloved choke. Tears soaked my face.

My mother stayed with me through the night because she knew that at any moment, Daryle could begin aspirating again. Of all the care I wanted to give my beloved, I simply could not do this, even in this critical stage. It was a long night as Daryle needed suctioning repeatedly, but the morning came as mornings do. We had preplanned a party for this beautiful May morning. My nephew Kacey turned twenty-one on May 5, 2013, so we decided to have the party at our house because everyone, especially Kacey, wanted to be near Daryle. Kacey is a great kid and will do anything for anyone. He loved his uncle Daryle. Daryle and Kacey shared a special bond as music buddies, movie buddies, and friends. They even had a special handshake that only the two of them did together. It was theirs and theirs alone. I wanted Daryle to know that everyone was coming for the party, so I said, "Honey, open your eyes. Look at me. We're having Kacey's twenty-first birthday party here." At this stage he barely had the strength to open his eyes, but they fluttered open for second. It was so incredibly hard to celebrate in the same room with what we all now realized was a dying man. We made sure Daryle could hear what was happening, but he never opened his eyes again and I believe he slipped into a coma while the many voices of his loving family surrounded him.

Death doesn't care if it's your twenty-first birthday. Kacey didn't want to be anywhere else. Even so, he never wanted to celebrate another birthday again, until I told Kacey one day that Uncle Daryle's last thoughts were of him. While Daryle lay unconscious, Kacey prayed the best prayer for me, asking God to help me in my dark hour. I have used that saying many times since then. It was ironic that Kacey wanted to be there for Daryle, but I think God was using Kacey to be there for me.

As daylight faded into twilight, I remember staring up through the skylight in our kitchen. I could see a faded moon in the deepening blue sky. I know I'm no poet, but I began to feel like I was floating as these words poured out of me:

"Beyond the Moon"

Peering through the big pale blue,
I think of you beyond the moon.
You hear my thoughts so far away,
Hear me now as I pray.
You gave us love and together our hearts,
Meshed so tightly never to part;
Hear me Lord from the depths of my soul,
As I have given you full control.
Leave my love on earth a bit more,
Your word is true, only YOU restore.
So as I glance up towards the moon,
I know someday you'll come here soon;
And we'll all go home with the groom,
As we ride with YOU beyond the moon.

The next day, May 6, 2013, we made phone calls to family and friends to invite them to speak in his ear on the phone or to come by the house. People brought food, sat around his bed, and sang to him. Ironically, we were still in the midst of bathroom renovation. I hadn't expected Daryle's decline to come upon us so quickly, so we found ourselves surrounded by intense activity as our hearts moved in slow motion. Rick was in New York. When I called him, he said with tears, "I can't watch him die, Mom." I was sitting next to Daryle as he began "Cheyne-Stokes breathing," a rhythmic waxing and waning of deep breathing as the body struggles for life. His sister and my daughter, sister, parents, son-in-law, and niece Taylor, along with many friends, all sat with me as Taylor prayed the most powerful faith-filled prayer. The room was saturated with faith.

I went into the bathroom to pray, "God, I don't know how much more he can take. I don't know how much more I can take. Please, help him." As I was walking back, he was in my line of sight and my daughter cried out, "Daddy!" and then "Mummy!"

I rushed to the bed and as I sat next to him, I heard his last breath escape from his lungs. I checked his eyes and they were fixed. I noticed the clock: 5:15 p.m.

I immediately turned and looked up and screamed, "Come back, honey! Please, come back."

Everyone screamed "NO! NO! God, NO!"

I thought, "God, it's all up to You now. I believe. I know his spirit is not here now, but You can bring him back!"

I asked someone to call Rick. When they returned, they said that Rick was in a boat when he received the call. He had just pushed off from shore because he wanted some alone time. As he floated out onto the lake, he saw a lone goose soar into the night sky and he knew. Daryle had felt like he was soaring before this final ascent, and I knew too that his spirit had finally flown to Heaven.

He was gone. I had been losing a little more of my Daryle each day for a year, but now I knew I had lost my big strong husband, my protector, my lawnmower, my travel buddy, my co-adventurer, my intimate partner, my personal musician and praise leader, my fishing companion, my yard sale pal, and so much more. It was exactly 365 days from Daryle's diagnosis that he died.

PART II

LIFE WITH LOSS

CHAPTER 9

THE WALKING DEAD

My grief was instant, deep, and devastating. I felt in that moment that I was just as dead as Daryle... dead, dead, dead... but somehow I was still alive. I remember walking around the bottom of Daryle's bed as he lay there lifeless. I had nothing left. I suddenly felt very heavy, heard a buzzing in my ears, felt my eyes roll back in my head, and I passed out. My son-in-law, Kevin, caught me and literally had to drag me to the bed in the other room. I could hear everyone talking but absolutely could not respond. I just had zero strength. I heard them trying to figure out how to help me. When the EMT's (emergency medical technicians) came to confirm Daryle's death, their concern shifted to me because I was unresponsive. I heard my mom say they would have to take me to the hospital if I didn't open my eyes. I thought, "Good. Maybe I will die there." I could hear everyone, but nothing they said made any impact on me.

I now found myself strangely like Daryle. I did not have the strength to open my eyelids. The EMT was taking my blood pressure, which was not good. He flashed his flashlight in my eyes, but I didn't flinch. My body felt like a cold cast iron shell. Though physically paralyzed, my spirit was strong and literally fighting to leave my body. I prayed in that frozen state, "God, let me out! Let me go! Take me home. I want to be with Daryle." I felt two distinct beings: the body, frozen, and the spirit, alive, and sensed what my hubby must have felt, but now he was free of his earthly bonds, truly soaring at last.

My spirit wanted to join Daryle in Heaven. I was half dead anyway. I felt like I was halfway there. I just couldn't find the exit. But then the Lord spoke to my heart. I heard nothing but His voice, though the physical room was filled with more than thirty sobbing and wailing people. All I heard was Him, not another sound from the room. He spoke softly and very gently, but ever so clearly, "It is not yet your time." The buzz of the room returned to my consciousness and, immediately out of my right ear, I heard my five-month pregnant daughter cry to her husband, "Not both my parents in the same day!" Well, if that doesn't get you, I guess you *are* dead! That snapped me back. I opened my eyes. She hugged me and we just sobbed and sobbed.

The only funeral home in our town was right down the road from our home. They arrived quickly, and I watched as they respectfully cared for my husband. As they were about to take him away, something rose within me. I jumped up as others tried to hold me back and threw myself onto Daryle's lifeless, cold body. Whispering in his ear, I pleaded, "Please, come back! Don't leave me, honey! I love you!" I watched them gently place my beautiful husband on a gurney, cover his body with a blanket to his neck, and wheel him down the stairs. I was struck, as if with a spiritual microburst, with the absolute finality of death. I knew I would never see him walk up these stairs again. Daryle was gone. This was undoubtedly the "third longest day."

I had been with Daryle for almost forty years. I had fallen in love with him as a teenager and had spoken with him every day since. We did everything and discussed everything together all the time. My Daryle was gone. I wanted to talk to him. I had a million questions. "What are you experiencing? Have you seen Jesus yet? Is my dad there? Do you see your brother, your dad? How's your knee? Is the scar gone from your head?" But I couldn't talk to Daryle. I was alone. I wanted to make all this go away. I wanted just one more minute with him, even if he was weak, sick, or in bed. I just wanted to hold his hand. Even if he couldn't talk back, I just wanted to talk to him. People who cared were all around me, but I just wanted my Daryle.

Family began flying in from all over. It was mayhem. Folks arrived from everywhere: South Carolina, Denver, and New York, including Darlene who had just left two weeks prior. We were trying to accommodate everyone. Friends let us borrow their camper. Folks stayed with me and my mom. Massive amounts of food were brought in. Funeral arrangements had to be handled. My nieces and their cousin were practicing to sing at his service. The plans and people and logistics overwhelmed me since I was barely functioning. I passed through all these activities like the walking wounded, wishing simply to be left alone in my sorrow. But no one would leave me alone, and finally the day came.

At the funeral, Rick stood up and said wonderful things about his dad, acknowledging it was much more difficult to speak than he thought it would be. Stephanie and I got up and addressed everyone. I wanted people who didn't know Daryle well to get a sense of him, so I asked those gathered to come up and tell stories about him that even I might not have heard. My Daryle would have been proud. One story was about a young man who hadn't seen Daryle in a long time, but he came to visit while he was sick. They were talking about life, and this man shared that he was struggling to pay his rent. Daryle reached into his wallet and gave him his secret stash that he'd saved up over many months, telling his young friend to take care of his rent. That was Daryle's heart for people. A little seven-year-old child also stood up to speak. He said a lot of things but the sweetest was simply, "Thank you Mr. Daryle for taking me fishing and to the beach. I love you forever, Mr. Daryle." Another said, "Thank you Mr. Daryle for teaching me guitar." One of the most meaningful comments was from a young man who'd been in our youth group. He said that hearing all these things about Daryle's life encouraged him to be a better man. Wow! Daryle's song, "Open Arms," played in the background at the end of the service. He'd recorded the song, and it was surreal to hear him singing at his own funeral.

Once we made it to the cemetery, I knew this was it… the last chance, the last opportunity for God to do a miracle. Once they put the coffin in the ground and covered it with dirt, it was done. I whispered, "God, if You're going to do it, now is the time!" I knew God resurrected Jesus and had even brought my friend David back to life after he'd been pronounced dead, and I got mad thinking that evil seemed to be winning. I wasn't ready to accept that and was believing God for a miracle any second.

The casket was closed because I wanted people to remember him the way he was. I had put a picture of Daryle and me on the casket. When asked why, I snapped "Don't you get it? I died with him!" They were getting ready to lower him and again, I experienced that rush and hurled myself onto the coffin with a red rose in my hand. I didn't care what anyone thought of me. Again, I reminded the Lord, "God, this is it." I intently listened, waiting to hear my love saying, "Um, can you open this?" Even though I didn't have a crow bar handy, you can bet I would have opened it! As we turned to go back to the long black limo, the finality of the moment overwhelmed me. I could not speak. That frozen feeling was creeping back in.

The days that followed are a bit blurry. I do know that in those first few days after Daryle's death, they came to reclaim all the equipment that had structured our world for the last year: the hospital bed, the Hoyer, the Foley, the walker, the meds, the breathing apparatus. It was all discarded or removed. Everything that I had used to help him was gone. I felt a weird bond to those things. They were part of our shared intimate experience and had become part of my identity, and they were being erased. It all happened so quickly. I was stunned and felt even more loss, if that was even possible.

I remember three days after Daryle died, I was in our bedroom in complete darkness, lying still. It was about 3:00 a.m. I wasn't crying or upset. I was still. Out of that darkness, I heard my husband's voice as clear as if he were sitting next to me, "I'm okay, I'm okay." I sat up and replied, "I know you're okay, but I'm not okay." I thought I was losing my mind because biblically, I'd never heard of anything like that, but it somehow brought me comfort.

One week after Daryle died, my best friend Michelle stayed over (apparently folks did not want to leave me alone). Around midnight I had gone up to bed. She was still downstairs when we heard tires squealing, then a loud crash. I came running downstairs, my heart racing, just in time to see a car taking off down the street. I noticed part of my fence going with him! I called the police and we soon discovered that whoever hit my stone wall and broke my fence had left their bumper in my yard. Thankfully the license plate was still on it! But they'd also wiped out half of the ancient rhododendron bush growing in my yard. As if my heart was not broken and my nerves were not frazzled enough, this symbol of lasting beauty, love, and history in my life had been torn in two. I thought, "No more! How do I survive this? Do I get a break?"

I thought that going through Daryle's death was the end of me, and that my life was very much over. I would now live as half a person. It felt like I was being pulled apart from head to toe. I was reminded of a childhood memory. My brother Paul used to have a wrestling action figure called "Stretch Armstrong." This toy came with a guarantee that no matter how you stretched it, he would always go back to his original shape. Naturally my brother and I put it to the test. We stretched him across table, tied him in knots and pulled him around corners, and then let him go with a snap. Sure enough, he would shrink back to his original size.

One day we stretched Stretch too far and ripped his leg off. We actually got to see what was on the inside. This got me to thinking about a scripture, "Consider it pure joy, my brothers and sisters, whenever you face trials of many kinds, because you know that the testing of your faith produces perseverance. Let perseverance finish its work so that you may be mature and complete, not lacking anything." (James 1:2–4, NIV) I wondered if it was God's plan to stretch me. I felt torn. When God stretches you, I believe you never go back to your original shape. You're not supposed to. You're purposefully altered. I felt my heart had been ripped apart, but I thought maybe God was revealing to me what was on the inside. I wanted to know why He allowed all this and what He wanted to draw out of me and pour into me.

In the meantime, the stretching left me feeling like all my nerves were exposed and raw. If anyone rubbed against me physically or came too close, I wanted to scream, and I often said, "Don't touch me!" As I read my daily devotional so many times, it was just perfect timing. "All my longings lie open before You, Lord; my sighing is not hidden from You. My heart pounds, my strength fails me; Even the light has gone from my eyes. My friends and companions avoid me because of my wounds; my neighbors stay far away." (Psalm 38:9–11, NIV) After reading this, I realized that I wasn't the first one to experience this excruciating pain. David had felt it too. In my mind I grasped that we all understand what it is to hurt, but this hurt felt like I'd been cut in half. Marriage had made us "one flesh" and that flesh had been torn in two, leaving me utterly alone and void.

During the next four months, I didn't give a rip what happened to me. I believe I lived in utter darkness, just stumbling from event to event, person to person, place to place. I couldn't imagine anyone saying anything that had any value, but my broken heart still whimpered, "Someone help me. Get me out of this." I was numb, and no human being brought me comfort. I was consumed by my own nightmare. There was no way to snap out of it. I couldn't understand how this could all really be happening to me. I was barely able to help myself, let alone try to comfort the people around me who had also suffered a great loss.

The affects of death aren't exclusive to the widow. The whole family suffers. I asked members of my family about their thoughts concerning Daryle's death. My brother Paul said it was the day the "real" George Bailey got his wings. Randy, my stepdad said, "My son-in-law and friend... his death was just like the song says. It was "the day the music died." Stephanie had declared, "It ain't over 'til it's over," believing with her husband Kevin that God could resurrect her dad until he was actually buried in the ground. They were devastated. Rick felt regret because his last words to his dad were, "I'm praying for your healing," but in hindsight he wished he had said,

"Dad, thank you for loving me." My mom cried out, "I've lost my son." Kacey shared that "Daryle was the finest example of an earthly father." My sister Tra said that "he was the kindest and best of men" and the Godliest man she had ever known. My niece Taylor had come to the house one day and found her uncle watching *The Hobbit – An Unexpected Journey.* When we lost Daryle, she realized her uncle had taken his own journey, but that his was final. Words spoken by Frodo came back to her,

> "How do you pick up the threads of an old life?
> How do you go on, when in your heart
> you begin to understand there is no going back?
> There are some things that time cannot mend
> Some hurts that go too deep, that have taken hold."

Daryle's journey home didn't comfort her or any of us. His loss had taken hold and produced crushing grief that only God could comfort.

My families in both Northern Ireland and in Canada were also torn apart. They hadn't been able to come to the funeral, so in June, one month after Daryle's passing, Steph, now seven months pregnant, Kevin my son-in-law, Michelle, my BFF, and I decided it would be a good distraction for me to cross the Pond back to my birthplace, Northern Ireland. We hoped the Irish and I could comfort each other. My sweet cousin Louise and her great hubby, Jim, welcomed us with open arms. Steph had been to Ireland with Daryle, but it was wonderful to show Michelle and Kevin my childhood stomping grounds. However, everywhere we went reminded me of my fun times with "my Cheese" and his now glaring absence on this trip. I knew this was not helping me and could feel myself withdrawing. Once again,

I was surrounded by people who loved me, yet all I wanted was to be left alone. If one more person said, "I'm so sorry for your loss," I was going to knock them out! In my head I was screaming, "You have no idea about my loss!" but out of my mouth came, "Thank you." I just felt like I was going through the motions, sleepwalking, hoping I would wake up and it would all be over. I was not myself, still trudging along in a fog somewhere between death and life.

I often refused to let my family talk to me. Even at church, if I heard one thing I didn't like, I would leave abruptly. There was a permanent new worship leader who obviously was *not* my Daryle. My Daryle had trained him and my Daryle was now gone forever. I was confronted with that fact every time I went to church. The place that had been my sanctuary, my home and my happy place was now a source of constant pain. I would tell people not to touch me. I wasn't eating, but my registered dietician daughter asked me if I could at least sip on water every day. And sleep? What was that? I just wanted to get in the car and drive. I had actually planned to leave town without telling anyone, but the Lord spoke to my heart revealing that wherever I went, I would be taking my pain with me, and I would still be alone, separated from my family and isolated with my pain.

The real problem was that I didn't want anyone to tell me what to do or how to feel. I finally felt like I had a say in my own affairs. I hadn't been able to control Daryle's life, and I didn't have a say in the outcome. For a year I had been in a medical prison, unable to leave my home or my patient's side. I wasn't mad at God, but I was getting mad at people trying to control my environment and my actions after they had all been determined for me for such a long time. Of course I knew in my heart that they just cared about me, but I had to sort out my next steps on my own. I just wanted everyone to leave me alone and nobody would, including God.

Sadly, within a few weeks, our family would suffer another loss. I have two cousins in this country, Lynne and her brother Scott. I got word that my cousin Lynne was dying from cancer. I went into the hospital to see her and had to visit her on the same floor that Daryle had been on. It was a physical challenge even to go into the room, but I kissed her on the cheek, told her I loved her, and she died one week later. When I left the hospital, I thought I was doing really well, but nope—meltdown! I understood that death is a part of life. I just didn't want to face anymore for a while. I pleaded with the Lord to help me through, the operative word being "through," because at this stage, I knew I did not want to get stuck there! I wanted to move on. I had to move on!

Pondering death can take us to dark places. I literally wondered, "Who's next?" Lynne was younger than me and Daryle. Her death overwhelmed and depressed me. I couldn't go to the funeral because I didn't have a grip on my emotions and knew I literally might pass out again. I was physically shaken for days after visiting Lynne in the hospital and felt physically sick as I wondered how many more of my people would have cancer and would have to die. Jesus was with me, but I still struggled with my thoughts and emotions.

Thank you, God, for not giving up on me! He encouraged me in a miraculous way on July 27, 2013. An evangelist came to speak at a special three-day meeting at our church. I'd briefly met him on my way out of church the first night of the event. The second night he was late, and as the guest speaker, his absence was noticeable. We later learned that he was late because he'd been arguing with God. The Lord asked him to do something at this particular service that he had never done in his ten years of ministry, namely, to write a letter to *me*, and to read it in front of the entire congregation! He said to the Lord, "No God, I don't want to. I don't even know that girl." But the Lord pressed him. So, on that life-changing day, he read aloud, saying, "This is for you, Mrs. Borrows:

> I know the pain hurts.
> I know the days are different.
> And it's all right to mourn and miss and shed tears.
> But today allow My strength to become your joy.
> You mentioned to my servant that it has been eleven
>   weeks and four days since you last heard your
>   husband's voice.
> Allow Me to be your comfort and peace.
> Allow Me to be your husband.
> I see you at sunrise.
> And when you lay your head to sleep, I see your tears.
> But joy is coming in the morning.
> Allow today, right now, to be your morning.
> Don't allow the enemy to steal your praise.
> Like my servant David said, 'Bless Me at all times,
> let my praise continually be in your mouth.'
> If you allow the devil to steal your praise,
> he will cripple you.
> But I say to you, let out praise unto Me
> and My supernatural peace will come upon you."

The words were obviously so specific to my circumstances that I knew it was from the Lord. I had actually stopped going to worship service because it was too agonizing. But here I was back at church, and the Lord wasted no time in telling me that if I let the devil steal my praise, it would cripple me. I realized I needed to get my act together, but that was easier said than done. I was still working through it and facing major milestones. I turned fifty while Daryle was sick. I became a widow at fifty. And I was about to become a grandmother at fifty.

In August of 2013, Steph and I went to a grief support group. She was nine months pregnant, but the meeting was held in a hospital so we would be safe if she went into labor! Sadly, it was in the windowless basement of the hospital, and all I could think was, "So is it the morgue?" We were crammed into a depressing little room with an overabundance of tables, and not a tissue box to be found in a room full of grieving human beings! I thought, "Are you kidding me? What kind of place is this?" No one really knew who the leader was, and it was kind of a free for all. They were talking about looking to psychics, mediums, and all kinds of things that God's Word specifically warns against. Steph put her hand on my leg and I prayed, "Lord, get us out of here!"

My heart went out to one little lady across from us who was clearly shaking and hurting. People rolled right over her as tears streamed down her cheeks. I knew these people could not help her, and that they wouldn't help me! I was dimly aware and surprised that my still frozen heart actually cared, at all, about what someone else was feeling. This was in stark contrast to my antisocial depression. I wanted to go over to hug her. She was suffering. How could everyone be so blind? The fleeting thought that I could actually help her crossed my mind and shocked me. I somehow sensed that God was moving in me, awakening my heart, and giving me a glimpse of my future calling. Well, Stephanie started going into labor right then and there, so we excused ourselves. Her contractions stopped as we discussed what had just happened. "Am I crazy or was that just awful?"

"No, Mom, it was awful!"

"I have a mind to start my own," I spouted.

"You should, Mom."

"Hmm, I will pray about it."

Two days later the real contractions began, and off to the hospital we went. We had just arrived when Stephanie went into hard labor. It was decided that she should go into the tub to relax her back muscles and ease her pain. As soon as she settled into the tub her water broke, and she wanted to push. Holy cow! The doctor had just left. They quickly called him back and at 8:02 p.m., my daughter gave birth to her precious baby girl, Madelyn Joy! The joy was bittersweet as I held her in my arms. My mind drifted once again to my Daryle and an excerpt of a book I'd read called *My Time in Heaven* by Richard Sigmund. As I cut the umbilical cord, I recalled the author's vision, "There are balconies and bleachers in heaven that look over the events on earth. People come to watch prayers come to pass. They are the 'cloud of witnesses' the Bible says it like this "Therefore, since we are surrounded by such a great cloud of witnesses" (Hebrews 12:1, NIV) People in heaven watch births and weddings on earth. They are a cheering section, hollering out encouragement to us." In the hope that Daryle was glancing over the balcony of Heaven, I held up the baby and said, "Here she is, Daryle. Madelyn Joy, our granddaughter." It was astounding to me that such incredible joy and such inexpressible sorrow could exist at the same time. I cried all the way home.

A month after Maddie's birth, we all ventured to Charleston, South Carolina, for my niece's wedding. I thought this might be good for me, but discovered once again, just as I had in Ireland, that I simply could not get away from "my Cheese." The last time I'd visited South Carolina, I was with Daryle. Everywhere I went I was flooded with memories of him. I was pretty sure one of these days I was just going to fall down dead from a broken heart! That is what it felt like. Even back at home, there were memories everywhere I turned. I thought, "That's it! Time for a change."

I decided to change everything in the house or else move. I do like where I live, so change the house it was. My HGTV genes kicked into high gear. First on the list: our living room where Daryle had spent his last months of life. I thought it would be easy. I thought wrong. It was a sunny yellow color, and I happily decided to paint it "Sandstone." But once I got to the very last patch of yellow, which was near the head of Daryle's bed, I couldn't bear to paint over it. So my mom, who had been helping me paint, took the brush from my hand and compassionately finished the job. I fell to my knees and cried uncontrollably. The definition of "meltdown": "a quickly developing breakdown or collapse: a sudden loss of control over one's feelings or behavior." Yes, that pretty much summed it up.

Redecorating is fun, right? Sort of, kind of, but changing our bedroom also turned out to be exceptionally difficult. It had been decorated in chocolate and turquoise, a nice balance of male and female, but I transformed the room into a feminine vision in white. I also added a Victorian-style chandelier. My 6'2" Daryle definitely would have hated it because he would have hit his head on it every day! It made me laugh to imagine him joking and complaining, and then of course it made me cry. Shabby Chic, Beachy Cottage is my style. I loved the changes and they helped me because I wasn't reminded of Daryle absolutely everywhere I looked. Completing the renovations was an important step toward accepting my circumstances and creating a new life.

I finally got to enjoy my brand-new shower, which also resulted in, you guessed it, another meltdown. This was the shower that I'd shown him in pieces. We were supposed to enjoy this shower and our refinished bathroom together. I'd designed it so that I could wheel his shower chair right into the stall, but now my Daryle was gone. He would never need this shower. He would never see this shower. So here I stood alone in this big new shower, which should have been, and genuinely was a blessing, and I just cried. "Ugh. How many of these am I going to have? How can a person cry this much? I am going to run out of tears!" In Psalms, God says He knows our sorrows and that He collects our tears. I thought, "My bottles of tears must be overflowing by now."

Experts tell us there are five stages of grief: denial, anger, bargaining, depression, and acceptance. I assume whoever came up with these experienced a death. I do remember being angry, but never with God. I know that scripture says, "The thief's purpose is to steal, kill and destroy. My purpose is to give them a rich and satisfying life." (John 10:10, NLT) I do believe my anger was directed at the thief, the enemy of our souls. Well, steal and kill yes, destroy almost, so Lord, what happened to a rich and satisfying life? Being brutally honest with myself, I realized He did not promise it would be with my Daryle.

Even so, it was hard to imagine that this could be God's plan for me. I thought to myself, what do I do? Do I seek after my own happiness to try to create my own rich and satisfying life or should I wait on my Lord to direct me? God's Word says, "But the widow who lives for pleasure is dead even while she lives." (1 Timothy 5:6, NIV) There's no satisfaction in living like that and I knew this would not be the life I would be happy with. I truly wanted what God wanted for me.

I was desperately trying to figure this all out as I continued my DIY demolition. I do remember welling up in anger one particular day as I tore the wall-to-wall carpet up in the living room. I was using the hammer to pop up the tack board along the wall, when I yelled, "I hate that I have to live this way!" I took that hammer and slammed it onto the floor over and over and over again. I knew this old floor was getting recovered, so I took all my frustration out on those hapless pieces of wood. There were plenty of dents, I'll tell you! And I was pleased with myself. I was angry at my current situation, and at the enemy, but my breakdown in this case was actually liberating! It felt good to lash out, which I hadn't done since Daryle's death.

My meltdowns came in response to memories. I was blindsided by resurging grief and anger during the most mundane activities. I refer to those now as "sniper attacks": shopping at the grocery store, cooking for one, doing laundry for one, getting gas, putting out the trash, getting mail addressed to Daryle. All these things and more sent me into a tailspin. I was trying to move forward, but every little thing reminded me that I had to live my life by myself, and I didn't like it.

My meltdowns also sprung up out of frustration as I tried to figure out the "WHY" of it all. You have to move on past the memories, past the pain, often without any real understanding. Only God could reveal the "why," or He might choose not to for reasons only He knows. Even with faith, it can be hard to accept not knowing why. All I knew was that I could not stay where I was because that was certain misery. I had to press forward. I looked to God for help because I did not know how to do this on my own. I was sure of one thing. God knows the beginning from the end. He knows the future, and He knew mine.

CHAPTER 10

Out of the Fog

I slowly began to come out of my funk. God was using people and circumstances to speak to me. One particular day in church (I think it was during the prayer time), I was just standing in my usual fog when my friend Debbie came up to me and said, "I feel impressed to tell you what God has laid on my heart."

"OK." In my mind I'm thinking, "Knock yourself out." I was not very thrilled to hear it.

"God sees that your heart is shredded. But He wants you to know that it's okay to mourn. He's going to give you a new ministry to give hope to those who have none. He will give you a new joy, a new hope, and a new future."

I remember somberly asking her, "What was wrong with the old one?"

Another time she approached Stephanie to comfort her with another word from the Lord: "I AM that I AM. I know that you are hurting now, but one day you will see the beautiful tapestry that I have woven. All I ask right now is that you trust Me." My thoughts on that were, "We are trusting you, Jesus, but we don't see what You see. All we see on our side of this tapestry are knots and frays and tattered pieces of our lives! Help us, God!"

It was still clear to me that no one on earth could help me. No one knew what to say to me. No one could help me snap out of it. I was becoming someone I did not recognize. Though I was making some progress, I felt hopeless. Though I tried to fly under everyone's radar, my family was getting increasingly worried about me. Neither my son, my daughter, my best friend, nor my mom were able to reach into that very deep, dark place. Despite all the pieces that God was bringing together: my newly decorated home, my trips to Ireland and North Carolina, my granddaughter's birth, God's letter from the visiting pastor, I *still* did not want to live in a world without Daryle. Who could fix that?

I felt like a walking sore that no one could heal, like a leper, I guess. You can't cure a leper with Band-Aids, and I needed a cure. Though the Prophet's letter and Debbie's words offered me some hope of a future, I still felt adrift in a large sea, afraid and alone. Even though some part of me knew that my God was big, I felt so little. My meek words were, "God. If you can hear me, I just can't see my way through. I don't know how to hold on." I wasn't suicidal, just confused as to why my simple words seemed to fall on deaf ears. I knew the way I was thinking was dangerous.

I made a conscious decision that I needed to change. I began to meditate on the positive things. I flooded myself with uplifting Christian television shows, encouraging Christian music, anything positive that I could find. I then began to concentrate on the God-given words that were spoken over me, beginning with the letter.

God used the words "Allow me...."

Allow Me? What a gentleman! I realized first of all that God was not rushing in and taking over my life. I still didn't want anyone telling me what to do. God tenderly waited for me to invite Him into my darkness in a deeper way. Only God could shine light into that dark place within me. I began to realize that God was already in the darkness waiting for me, inviting me to come closer to Him. I was safe. I was okay, no matter what shape I was in. Nothing in my behavior would cause Him to push me away. He drew me closer.

The words in that letter began to burn off the impenetrable fog in my soul. I understand now, of course, that this letter was not just for me, but for any widow suffering the loss of their love. It certainly did something to me. Not too many people are granted a personal letter from God, so I knew I should take it seriously. The more I read it, and studied it, the more I felt His love and warmth in the depth of my being. He was loving me and I received it. I grasped at last that He had been trying to bring comfort to me all along. He was relentlessly reaching out toward me. But I had not been able to receive. At last I agreed to a reckoning with my Jesus. I didn't know what would be required of me or what it would mean, but I was finally able to say, "OK, God. Do what You do."

I was truly humbled as I thought about how He'd put up with me. God's Word calls it long suffering. He'd shown me such loving kindness and I had to wonder, "Why me?" I realized the answer. Out of the comfort I'd been given, God wanted me to minister His goodness and love to others. I understood that so many have suffered the same grief that I'd experienced, and even worse. They needed to know that there was a God who intimately loved them and wanted to comfort them.

I did not snap out of the fog of grief overnight. My fog acted more like the real thing on a grey day. One morning during my devotional time, I gazed out my kitchen window. A dense fog rested on the treetops. The fog slowly thinned, then the sky lightened bit by bit, and here and there the sun peaked through until the heat of the sun burned off the fog and the sky cleared. My constant companions: confusion, fear, deep sorrow, disorientation, and loneliness began to dissipate. The veil had been lifted. Looking back, I began to recognize that God had been with me all along. In retrospect, I saw His hand in the smallest things, especially the new bundle of life, Maddie Joy, who was an immediate treasure. I saw a glimpse of my husband in this precious gift. From birth, she did this funny little thing where she stuck her thumb in between her two middle fingers just like Daryle always did. Incredible! I knew he was in there! New life is a beautiful thing, and her life made me recognize that I needed to make some hard decisions about my own.

I decided it was time to help other people. I wondered who I could help the most and started a group for widows called the Widows Circle. We met once a month and became friends along the way. We shared our feelings, tears, and fears. I reminded them that if we let it, our grief can become our grave. We have to keep moving forward no matter the challenges. Some of those challenges were, for instance, the problem of "wedding rings," which is a biggie to new widows. "To wear or not to wear?" that was the question. It is a very personal choice. Some ladies never want to remove them and feel married even after their loss. I on the other hand felt like I had no right to wear what had been part of my union with Daryle. It was over, sealed. I was no longer married and just couldn't act like I was. That's me. I decided to have my jeweler make my engagement ring into a necklace. It looked beautiful; as I wore it I felt close to Daryle, just in a different form. Win/Win.

Another topic we discussed was not being able to sleep in our own beds. Goodness, the seemingly simple things were so tough! Well, I shared that I felt that the enemy of our souls had robbed us of enough. This was my house, not his; my bed, not the enemy's; every inch of this home was mine by God's grace, and he (satan) was not going to get one bit of it! I could feel my fighting Irish rising up, saying, "To battle, ladies! No more giving up or giving in! We can't be powerful and pitiful at the same time!" (I love that quote by Joyce Meyer).

Many of the widows struggled with finding out unpleasant things about their husbands after their deaths. In life, and after death, forgiveness is for our benefit, not our husbands'. Even the medical community has documented the health benefits of forgiveness and the toxic effect of bitterness. Another Joyce Meyer quote is, "Being angry at someone is like drinking poison and expecting the other person to die!" Well, it's doubly tragic to be unforgiving toward someone who's already gone and to let the poison of unforgiveness ruin your own life. But most importantly, even if we didn't understand all that, we simply needed to remember that the Lord forgave us and we must forgive. There is a freedom that comes when we forgive.

I used to think that whatever I was going through early on in my marriage was a big deal, but after Daryle's death, perspective kicked in and my worries and aggravations seemed insignificant. We all have battles somewhere along the way in marriage. We obviously get upset about the weightier issues, but we can foolishly get upset by the smallest things like, "You can remember who had the most homeruns in 1978 for the Red Sox, but you can't remember the five things I asked you to get from the grocery store?" Lots of us quarrel over little things that seem like big things. Clothes on the floor used to drive me crazy. I'd gripe, "You can ball up your clothes and 'shoot' them towards the hamper, but if you miss the floor is now their home!" Oh, what I wouldn't give to have those socks all over the floor again. We need to let go, choose our battles, and be peacemakers, because there is no going back. Death is just so absolute, so final.

Cleaning out our hubbies' belongings is especially hard because of the absolute heart-wrenching finality. Every item screams, "He will never need this again. He will never wear this again. You will never see him in this again!" Daryle wore huge, steel-toed, hardworking man boots that testified to how faithfully he provided for us, and suddenly they had no purpose. Some women can never face this task. I did it as soon as I was mentally and physically capable. Surprisingly, I discovered new things about myself as I faced this particular trial. As I purged my life of his stuff, I realized that the only stuff in my bedroom was mine and mine alone. I also realized that I had never had my own bedroom and, well, I kind of liked it.

When widows make changes they often feel guilty, because they feel like they're erasing their husbands' memory or dishonoring them in some way. I felt guilty for making my room "girly," but I loved it at the same time. I could just hear him saying, "What's a duvet?" Ha! I also discovered I was a bed hog, now sleeping on both sides of the bed when before I'd always stayed in my lane! I know he would have teased me for that too. And I'm sorry, but now that I had the bathroom all to myself, I liked it! I say all these things in jest, because oh Lord, I would have given it all up to have him back for a day.

Hindsight is 20/20 and I now realize that widows face a unique challenge of glorifying their lost loved ones. Even in a good relationship the people we lose are not saints, and we run the risk of elevating them to sainthood, thus creating an additional problem for any prospective love that follows. Some even create shrines to their spouses or refuse to move their belongings. For example, if their glasses were always left on the end table, that's where they will remain forever. Who can fill those perfect shoes? No one. These "little" habits all shout, "There's no room for you!" to anyone who might follow. Widows have to be careful not to close themselves off from future love because they've set the bar impossibly high based on idealized memories of their spouse. I had to be honest with myself as I was tempted to idolize Daryle. God tells us not to put anyone before Him, and I knew I needed to keep my rosy memories in check. Keeping ourselves in check in the midst of our heartache is the last thing we feel like doing.

Another really difficult problem many widows face is that their own bodies fail them after the death of their husbands'. Some women get chronic fatigue, insomnia, rapid heart rate, high blood pressure, intestinal problems, and more. I fell into this category. I did recover from my collapse following Daryle's death, but over the following months I developed serious medical issues that needed attention, including one that hospitalized me. Each time I went into the ER, the doctor would ask me, "Are you suffering from stress?" I routinely answered, "My husband just died. Does that count?" They would immediately bring in a social worker to counsel me, which only annoyed me more. I learned quickly that the hospital could only try to help the body; they couldn't do anything for my aching soul.

Doctors want grieving widows to de-stress by exercising, eating right and reexamining our choices to see if we are compounding our own problems. I'm a bit feisty by nature (remember "I can find my own seat!"), but I had learned to let go of the little things. The real problem was that widowhood caused me to crash against the wall of my own limitations and strength. I had been independent from a young age but realized now that I could only make it by depending on the Lord and His strength. He said He would be my husband and my strength. Well, as I called on Him to be just that, He answered every time. Though I didn't always see it as it was happening, God always came through for me throughout my life and throughout this horrible loss. Understanding this, I began to actually have fun seeing Him at work.

PART III

NEW LIFE

CHAPTER 11

DIVINE AWAKENING

> "The Spirit of the Lord God is upon me, because the Lord has anointed me to bring good news to the poor; He has sent me to bind up the brokenhearted, to proclaim liberty to the captives, and the opening of the prison to those who are bound;...to grant to those who mourn in Zion, to give them a beautiful headdress instead of ashes, the oil of gladness instead of mourning, the garment of praise instead of a faint spirit."
>
> (ISAIAH 61:1, 3, ESV)

We always believed for life, but Daryle's new life was in Heaven. God still had work for me to do, and I began a new life here. Spiritually something was brewing in me. I just knew it. I could sense it. I knew in my heart I was changing at last. God was trying to bring out of me what He alone had planted within me. Thinking of the many things spoken over me, I started to get excited about when something, anything, would happen, and I felt that if it didn't soon, I would burst.

The first step in my new journey was that our family prayerfully agreed that our season at Lighthouse Church was over. In order to enter into the new life God prepared, we sadly had to leave what we'd known and loved. We sensed that the Lord was moving us on, even though Pastor John had a heart of gold and had been very good to us. However, when God says, "Move," you move, even when you don't completely understand why. I did understand that whatever God was about to do simply could not be done if we remained. This decision ushered in a very different life. The Lord opened up a new church, new friendships, and new opportunities for us. I am a person who likes change, but wow, there were so many in such a short time it was dizzying. The reason you are reading this book was due to that change.

I had no clue what was about to happen to me. I prayed for God's clear direction and understanding. God provided a special answer to prayer through trusted friends whom I'd known for thirty years—Reverend David and Kathy Walker. They are evangelists who have an incredible story. David was known as the boy preacher, "Little David." He was healed of blindness at age five, and at age sixteen was raised from the dead after a drowning accident. The Walkers have written several books and together have travelled the world preaching the Good News. David heard from the Lord and once told my mom that she would get married again. He also told her that she already knew her future husband. Mom was skeptical but sure enough, she and Randy, a former friend from church, have been married since 1989! I saw David's prophecy come true before my own eyes, and there had been many more accurate words of knowledge that the Lord gave to us through him.

This extraordinary couple were surrogate parents to us, and Daryle had loved them both dearly. Unfortunately they were unable to be with us when Daryle died, but they visited some months later. I told the Lord on a beautiful September day during their stay, "If You have anything to say to me, I will hear it from David. I trust him." I didn't know if the Lord would answer me, but as my family prepared to have lunch out on the deck, David and I stood in the kitchen. He looked at me and said, "We have to talk."

"Okay. Now?" I asked.

"No. After lunch."

I told everyone, and you can bet we all ate pretty quickly.

David finished his meal, and you could have heard a pin drop. He looked at me and said, "The Lord has put it on my heart to tell you that in a couple of years there will be a major change coming to your life."

I replied, "David, my life has already had a major change."

He took my arm and said, "Yes, but this is a really good one."

I pondered that for a second and said with a giggle, "Is that all you've got?"

He also replied with a giggle, "That's all I've got!" He mentioned the story in the Bible about the Road to Emmaus and told me to start walking and praying. He told me to read Luke 24 and assured me that God would give me clarity.

"Okie dokie. That is what I will do." David's few words gave me a lot to chew on.

The Lord says, "Come close to God, and I will come close to you." (James 4:8, NLT) I became so curious about God's promise that I found myself spending more and more time with Him. You know the Bible is absolutely amazing! As I depended on God and sought Him *because* of my broken heart, He not only healed my heart, He showed me so much about Himself, things I'd never grasped before. It's not like I wasn't learning while Daryle was alive. It's just that now I wanted to know more and more about the One who said He wanted to "be my husband." That meant so much to me. I began to trust Him, rely on, lean on, and press into Him wholeheartedly. Words fail. I cannot explain how in tune I was with God's plan for me at this point. Whatever He asked me to do, wherever He asked me to go, I was ready, willing, and able. I trusted Him completely no matter what.

We celebrated Madelyn's baby dedication, a small ceremony in which we as her family commit ourselves to bringing her up to know Jesus as Lord and Savior. It was both a happy and sad day because it was the six-month anniversary of Daryle's death. I kept thinking, "I'm doing good, I'm doing good." I was looking forward to the day and having about thirty guests for lunch. On this special day, I got up early to get ready. Our kitty, Chloe, was at the end of my bed when I awoke, and she raced me downstairs as usual. I suddenly heard hacking and thought, "Oh, great! She's going to hack up a fur ball just in time for one of my guests to step on it!" But as I headed downstairs, I saw her lying motionless on our sun porch. I knew right away that she was dead! "NO! Chloe. NO! No, God, NO." She was only six years old! "Lord, are you seriously kidding me right now? How much more can I take? Not today of all days!"

Chloe wasn't just any cat. She was like a "service" cat—you know, just like a service dog? She was more like a dog in a cat suit than a traditional cat. When Daryle was dying I put her on him, and after he died I put her on him again. She smelled him, looked at me, jumped down, came over, and never left my side from that day on. She always came when I called her and slept with me every night. She knew that if she sat with me, I felt better. Animals sense these things. She was so funny, she made me laugh. She adored a little stuffed puppy which she carried around in her mouth just like her own kitten. Wherever she dropped it, I would find it and play a game of hide and seek with her. I took the puppy from her secret hiding place and would gasp, "Where's your puppy?" She would literally perk up her head, get up, look around, and search until she found it. She then picked it up by the scruff of its neck just like it was a real kitten and would drop it at my feet.

When we rescued Chloe, she was smaller than her beanie baby puppy. I fed her with an eyedropper until she was strong enough to eat on her own. I took care of her when she needed it, and she had comforted me when I needed it, which made her death sting all the more. Because of Madelyn's dedication, I was surrounded by family in this awful moment. Thankfully the men got out their shovels and buried her for me. I laid my beloved furry baby to rest with her puppy nestled in her arms. I was so raw already, and this just ripped another gash in my soul. I was bombarded with other losses at this time as well. My washing machine broke down. My car died. I made a declaration that if one more thing died under my care, I was going to give up!

God graciously gave me a respite from trouble as I sought Him continually. Before I knew it, I found myself talking to my "heavenly husband" about an important day in November. "My birthday is tomorrow, Lord, and last year was so special. Father, I just need to know that You are hearing me. You mentioned that You would be my husband and, well, my husband would give me a gift for my birthday. That's what I'm asking for: a candy bar, flowers, gum, anything from someone who doesn't know it's my birthday." The next morning, I awoke and said, "Good morning, Lord. Thank you for my birthday." I got ready and went to work.

Three hours later I received a phone call. "Mrs. Borrows, this is your jeweler. Remember when we made your ring into a necklace?"

"Yes, my family loved it. Thank you."

"Oh great, but that's not why we're calling."

"Oh … okay."

"When you were here you put your name in the jar for the drawing we were having."

"Oh, gosh. That was so long ago I forgot."

"Well, you won. You won the grand prize."

"What? Seriously? You don't understand. It's my birthday!"

"Well: happy birthday!"

"Wait, what did I win?"

"You won a $900 Tourmaline and diamond necklace."

"I don't even know what Tourmaline is, but I'm sure I will love it. Thank you."

I bolted down there and they put it on my neck. It was gorgeous. Shaped in a square with a "pink" (girly) stone surrounded by diamonds—wow! I asked God for a candy bar and He gave me eye candy! My Heavenly Hub is alright! I wore it so proudly because it wasn't a piece of jewelry. It was proof of God's love and proof that He was at work in my life. No one on this planet could ever convince me that this was not a gift straight from Him. He not only heard but He answered in a big, visible, unbelievable way that left me saying, "Only God!"

I felt as if the Bible were coming to life. I was watching it happen. I love this scripture: "Now all glory to God, who is able, through His mighty power at work within us, to accomplish infinitely more than we might ask or think." (Ephesians 3:20, NLT) I was about to see exactly what that meant as I headed off to a much-needed Ladies Retreat. This was an annual get-together I had enjoyed for many years. Donning my necklace, I floated through the day feeling loved and delighted with what my Jesus had given me for my birthday.

We went to different classes during the retreat and loved each one, but two were especially significant to me. In the first, the woman speaking was a beautiful little Italian spitfire named Jody. She told us a story about the Lord giving her a nickname. She felt He had called her "Butterfly." Her response was, "Butterfly? Well, if that's true, Lord, then have three of them fly past me before I leave this golf course" She walked on the course for a couple of hours and nothing. She thought she had lost her mind, but then as she put her key into her driver's side door, a butterfly flew past her hand. "What? No way!" Then as she got in the car, two more went by the windshield. "Well, okay. I guess I'm not crazy. Butterfly it is."

She explained straightforwardly that in her life she had gone through many struggles but without them, she wouldn't be who she was today. She went on to say that when the Lord wants to get her attention, or just show His loving thoughts toward her, somehow a butterfly is involved. As she turned around, she said, "See what I mean?" The entire stage had been decorated for the retreat, and on all the columns were giant butterflies. "It's nonstop," she said. "That's our God. Just ask Him if He has a nickname for you."

I thought, "That is so cool. I'm going to do it." It reminded me of how personally God had already spoken to me. On a recent walk I had my headphones on, and I was just relishing the hot sun beaming down on my face. I felt this prompting to turn off my headset, so I did. Then I said, "Lord, did you want to speak to me?" I heard in my heart, "You brighten My day, and I made the sun." My bottom lip quivered, because I knew I would not speak such things to myself. All I could think was, "Thank you, my Jesus. Thank you." What a boost to my heart. God was loving me and talking to me just like a loving husband…just like Daryle.

The other significant event that day came when I went to hear another woman's testimony. At the end of her session, this teacher asked anyone who wanted prayer to come down to the front. Well, I was always in need of prayer! About twenty of us went forward. I stood silently praying and listening to her pray for others. As I listened, I knew this woman was hearing from God. She pinpointed the ladies' intimate needs. I prayed, "Lord, what do you want to say to me? I'm listening."

As the speaker prayed for person after person, I thought maybe I should not have come up because she kept passing me by. My friend was with me and eventually, we were the only two left. Then the speaker prayed for my friend and as I listened, I realized her prayers mentioned something that my friend and I had just discussed privately the previous night in our room ... something only God and we knew. I was stunned. "God, You are great!" Finally it was my turn and I told her that my husband had died and yet how good God had been to me. I showed her His beautiful necklace. She put her arms around me and said, "Not that the others are not important to God, but He saved the best for last." She continued to say that I had no idea what God was about to do, and that there was so much that He had in store for me. "The necklace was the tip of the iceberg. Get ready. Keep preparing, He is not done with you." Talk about being blown away! I needed to hear from God and to feel His presence, and He did not disappoint. I think I floated through the rest of the convention.

About a week after the retreat, I was in my bed and remembered what Jody had said about asking the Lord about a nickname. I had never heard anything like this in my thirty-plus years of being a Christian, but I was finding that truly, "nothing is impossible for God!" (Luke 1:37, CEV) I sheepishly asked, "Do you have a name for me, Lord?"

As I sat quietly on my bed I heard, "Flower."

I asked, "Flower? Do you mean like baking flour or smelly flower?"

Answer: "Smelly."

Okay; well, that was interesting. I started to do a little research. Ready? My birth name, Suzanne, means "Lily of the Valley," which is a flower! When I visited Daryle's grave our combined headstone had a guitar to commemorate him and a flower for me. I was born flower, and I will be flower when I go home to heaven. The definition of flower is: "1. The seed-bearing part of a plant. 2. The finest individuals out of a number of people or things, best, finest, pick, choice, cream, crème de la crème, elite." My middle name, Margaret, means "Pearl," which is defined as: "1. A hard, lustrous spherical mass, typically white or bluish-gray, formed within the shell of a pearl oyster or other bivalve mollusk and highly prized as a gem. 2. A precious thing; the finest example of something. The word pearl has become a metaphor for something very rare, fine, admirable, and valuable."

It is incredible to see how differently we view ourselves from how God sees us. He sees us through Jesus, the Perfect One. I said yes to Jesus years before, and He was and is my covering. I do not see myself as all of the things contained in those definitions, but I thought I have been "seed bearing" all my life. I had to laugh at the spherical mass. Hmm, time to go on a diet! But then I found out that pearl is also the name of a Hawaiian flower! Who knew? This was mind-blowing for me because, as you will soon read, God has used my nickname in many ways! I love Him!

I began to wonder, "What have you planted in me, Lord? I can feel it beginning to grow. I am beginning to feel new." Can anything come from these ashes? I recalled God's word again, "Now to Him who is able to do immeasurably more than all we ask or imagine, according to His power that is at work within us." (Ephesians 3:20, NIV) His Word was coming true. He was doing immeasurably more than I could ask or imagine. This was getting exciting! As I rolled through the holidays I had more meltdowns, but was finding that they were becoming less severe. At least I could see peanut butter (Daryle's favorite) in the store without completely losing it! I could be thankful at Thanksgiving, and I was able to receive the love of family and God at Christmas. Happy New Year? Not sure about that. Could I really be happy yet? Hmm, "better" yes, but happy? God was getting me ready, but there was still a lot of work to do.

CHAPTER 12

From the Ashes

God faithfully lifted the fog in my soul and He was about to do even more amazing things in my life. I find God often reveals spiritual truths through natural events. He often reveals His supernatural presence through physical circumstances. I now lived alone in a home and was responsible for all the care and upkeep. This can be an overwhelming burden and huge challenge for widows. There were two very large trees that dominated our backyard. They were rotting and needed to come down. I called the tree guys to give me an estimate on Friday. They promised they would come by Monday to do the job. Great. Well, they were a no-show, so a week later I called again. Still nothing. It was so frustrating that I wasn't making any headway with these guys. Daryle would have taken care of it in a minute. After a month it dawned on me, "Wait a minute. Lord, You said You would be my husband, and this is something my husband would have handled, so I'm giving it to You." The very next morning I awoke to a racket wondering, "What is that noise?" I peeked out the window and to my surprise, the tree guys were driving into my backyard and one was already in the tree! I did an air High Five to the Lord! He is so awesome!

I was 100 percent dependent on God. Because of the great need I still felt, I spent a great deal of time talking to God and reading His Word. As I sat in the quiet of the morning with Him, a feeling of deep calm would come over me. This was God's presence, and I just didn't want to leave this incredible peace. It was almost tangible, and it was slowly restoring and reviving my soul. God used my dependence and my need to deepen my trust and our relationship. He was with me and preparing me for the future He had planned for me. I was coming back to life.

Unfortunately, sometimes as we make progress dealing with our grief and we begin to feel like we're doing okay, the enemy of our souls strikes back, often harder than before. He doesn't want to lose his hold on us. He doesn't want us to experience wholeness, healing, or closeness to God. I was headed upstairs to bed one night and as I stepped onto the third step, the enemy whispered in my ear, "Your husband will never walk up these stairs again." I sat there for over an hour heaving and wailing as if I'd just lost Daryle. I begged God to take the pain from me. Finally, I got myself upstairs. I dropped into bed still wearing clothes, shoes and all, and sobbed. Before I could fall asleep, I physically felt a gentle brush across my cheek, like a hand or a wing. I wasn't startled at all, but instead felt a sweet peace come over me … a peace I could not drum up for myself as I lay there. I knew God was with me trying to comfort me.

The very next day my friend Vicki just "happened" to send me this little devotional she had read entitled, "It's Okay to Cry" which said,

"My Princess, I see how hard you try to handle your heart, and I know you want to live a life without heartaches or pain. I'm asking you to take a step closer to your Father in Heaven by crying out to Me when you hurt. Let Me heal you. Remember My chosen, King David? He cried out to Me in his fears, disappointments, and sin, and I answered. You are also My chosen one, and you are My daughter … so it's Okay to cry. I don't expect you to pretend that pain is not real. It is truth and tears that will give you the freedom that I want you to know. Now let go of that part of your heart that only I can heal. Let your heavenly Daddy hold you while you cry.

Love,

Your King *who wipes away your tears.*"

'Those who sow in tears will reap with songs of joy.'"

(Psalm 126:5, NIV)

No one could ever tell me that wasn't God's heart and healing hand stretched towards me. I had just experienced this very thing the night before. Good meltdown. Thank you, my Jesus.

The widow's walk is sometimes one step forward, two steps back. Not all my meltdowns were good. One day I'd just had it. I screamed, "I'm sick of feeling like 'here comes the lonely widow.' I'm sick of taking out the trash. I'm sick of having to go down to the basement to do dumb stuff. I hate raking leaves and mowing. I hate dragging 40 lb. bags of salt down to the water tank." In a snit, I dragged my garbage to the garage. As I angrily yanked the garage door handle upward, I hyperextended my pinkie. It swelled, turned purple, and I thought I'd broken it. I ran into the house scrambling for ice, which I didn't have, so the only thing available was a bag of frozen blueberries. They'd frozen together into a block of ice, so I smashed the bag. Though the berries loosened with the first whack, I smashed it again... and again... and again, screaming, "Why did he have to die? I hate this! I hate my life!"

My poor mother witnessed the fiasco and all I could do was bellow, "Mom, go home! Just leave me alone!" I cried so hard that my eyes swelled up (along with my finger), so I sat down in my chair and transferred the "Blueberry" ice pack to my eyes. Little did I realize that my repeated smashing had created a hole in the bag, so unbeknownst to me, blueberry juice began to mingle with the tears dripping down my face. I realized too late that blueberry juice now stained my cheeks, my arm, my clothes, and my new light-blue chair! It was everywhere! Having had enough, I decided to shut the house down and to go to bed at a sunshiny 4:00 in the afternoon. As I stomped into my bedroom, I grabbed a hold of my white duvet cover to give it a little fluff. The gust of air knocked my picture off the wall onto my ankle. My goodness... I'd had it!

The next day, God adjusted my attitude. I went into the grocery store in the rain, behind a little woman pushing a walker just like Daryle's. I learned she had incurable MS that she couldn't do anything about, just as I couldn't do anything about Daryle's death and my miserable condition. Realizing that her circumstances in the present moment were infinitely harder to handle than mine instantly humbled me and diffused the bombs blowing up inside me. I prayed with the woman right there in the parking lot, asked my mother to forgive my outburst, and cried out to God, "Forgive me for carrying on. Please forgive my blueberry meltdown." Lesson learned... I was convicted that no matter what I was going through, it could be worse.

Even though the Lord's touch was very real, I still felt the ache of loneliness. This hit me especially hard at dinnertime. Cooking for one was not fun, but I'd gotten used to it... sort of. One night I cooked a dinner of cubed chicken, garlic, and spinach. As the delicious aroma filled my kitchen, deep sorrow filled me as I realized I had no one to share this moment or this meal with, so I prayed, "I don't know why, Lord, but I don't feel like eating all by myself tonight. I guess I'm lonely. Would you send someone to be with me?"

Dinner was ready. I brought it to the table and prayed again, "Okay, Lord, then I guess it's You and me." I raised my fork to my mouth and glanced to my left, and out my window I noticed a bobbing head coming up my stairs. I quickly put my fork down, ran to the door, opened it, and saw my mom.

She was in her robe and pajamas and said, "Okay, what's going on? I was all comfy in bed and the Lord prompted me to come over here." Meltdown! She ended up having dessert with me. How absolutely good, amazing, and kind is our God?

God has comforted me over and over as Abba Father, meaning "Daddy," and as Jesus, my heavenly husband. I finally knew I was not alone even in the midst of tears and trouble. For He Himself has said, "I will never leave you nor forsake you." (Hebrews 13:5, ESV) And that "God is our refuge and strength, always ready to help in times of trouble." (Psalm 46:1, NLT) His overflowing loving kindness makes me question why *everyone* wouldn't want my Jesus. He wants to be your Jesus! He'd proven to me that no matter what I faced, I would never have to face it alone, ever! This was comforting to know. God was with me and working in me. I knew it and I was increasingly eager to keep pressing in and pushing forward toward His plan for my life.

Who knew God's plans included public speaking? I was

unexpectedly asked to speak to women at the local prison and then the Lord opened the opportunity to speak in church. I eagerly jumped in, thinking, "Okay, Lord, here we go." I preached about ten messages there, my very first entitled "Coming Out of the Fog" and my last entitled "When Resolution Becomes Revolution." I was increasingly aware that I had come to a new place. I was committed to whatever God wanted for me. I was suddenly fearless. I knew God held my hand. He had my back. He was walking me into my future. He had given me a new sense of boldness and excitement, which I hadn't felt in a long time. When you are resolved to do whatever God wants, your life will be revolutionized. Every time I stood before a group, the words just gushed out of me. I sat back, amazed as God went to work in me and through me. I knew He was bringing me full circle when I was asked to speak to the women's group at Christian Fellowship Center, the very church where I'd been saved, served, worked, been married, and had dedicated my children during the previous thirty years. One thing led to another and I was invited to speak at a Women's Aglow event. This is where God really got my attention.

I was in the hotel with my mom, going over my presentation. Suddenly, I had a meltdown. I cried to my Mom, "Why am I telling a room full of complete strangers about the absolute worst time in my life? What was wrong with me? God, You can't be serious."

My poor mom just came over, saying, "It's okay," as she patted me on the shoulder and prayed for me.

"Okay, Mom. I'm okay. Let's just do this and go home."

I had committed to speak so I went to the meeting. I remembered my promise to God that I would go where He sent me. After I arrived, the women's leader got up, went to the windowsill, and grabbed a vase that had some pretty purple flowers in them. She asked, "Does anyone know what type of flower this is?"

"Nope," I thought, "just purple." (I have a black thumb.)

"This flower is called the 'Obedience' Flower," she said as she walked over and handed them directly and only to me.

"Are you kidding me, God? Really?" My mom looked at me and I looked at her and we laughed.

I got the message, "Just be obedient, my little flower. I know what I am doing."

"Yes, Lord. Obedience. Got it."

The Bible says, "Whatever you do, work at it wholeheartedly as though you were doing it for the Lord and not merely for people." (Colossians 3:23, ISV) In Deuteronomy chapter 5 we are told to walk in obedience, and God continued to confirm His words and His thoughts toward me. Once again He was speaking directly to me, and every word was strength and healing to my soul.

As God restored me, He blessed me. I was having more and more fun babysitting my granddaughter. She was such a little miracle and I felt His presence every day through her. I was so conscious of the cycle of life. I had lost Daryle but was so grateful for this new life and the blessing that she was to the whole family. I know Daryle would have loved on her so much. He was always on my mind and I still wanted to share everything with him.

To the outside world, it must have looked like I was getting on with my life. As I went about my business, it must have seemed that my grief subsided. It's easy for the world to forget how much we continue to hurt. Despite God's constant comfort and guidance, I still cried my eyes out as I laid my head down at night. I felt like a hypocrite grieving privately while putting on a good face publicly. I knew that He says in His word, "There is a time for everything, and a season for every activity under the heavens: a time to weep and a time to laugh, a time to mourn and a time to dance." (Ecclesiastes 3:1, 4, NIV) I longed to move beyond mourning. God's Word had come alive to me, but knowing His Word isn't an instant remedy for everything that ails us. It's the cure held out before us, and we must choose it every minute of every day when we are in the thick of the trial.

The ever-present ache in my heart still left me feeling supersensitive, and one day someone made a stinging comment to me about Daryle's death. God rushed in with a human hug when I went to church the next day. A woman came up to me and said, "I thought of you yesterday and picked this up for you." It was a flower calendar, with a different flower every month! Hmm, coincidence? "Thank you, my Jesus, yet again, for showing Your love to me and revealing Your intimate involvement with every aspect of my life. Thank you that You care so much about the smallest hurt that You would send someone to comfort me." It reminds me yet again of His word: "How precious are your thoughts about me, O God. They cannot be numbered!" (Psalm 139:17, NLT)

Thanksgiving was coming around again. I was going to have company for ten days, including two Thanksgiving meals! I asked the Lord, as I would have asked my husband, to help me with my to-do list. "My Jesus, Keurig Coffee is crazy expensive. Would you please get that for me?" Well, I went to my friend Jan's house. She and her husband Dan are the kindest, most generous people, and on this afternoon as I put my coat on and threw my bag over my shoulder getting ready to leave, she said, "Wait, can I help you with anything for your Thanksgivings?"

"Nope," I said, completely forgetting about my morning prayer, "I think I'm all set, but thanks."

Halfway out the door, she chimed, "Well could you use some coffee? I have lots and I want to help out."

I left with five boxes of K-cups and giggled all the way home. I couldn't physically see God, but He was hearing me and continually providing for me, often through His people, but in ways they never suspected. People rarely realized how their choices and my prayers intersected, but God was at work in extraordinary ways. He was there as my husband as He promised in Isaiah. "For your Maker is your husband, the Lord of hosts is his name." (Isaiah 54:5, ESV)

I continued to move forward toward my first wedding anniversary without Daryle. As widows know, every approaching anniversary or holiday or birthday is an emotional mountain we face. On this Valentine's, *my* first anniversary alone, I wasn't sure how I would get through it. I didn't want to be swallowed up by this seemingly unending grief. I was determined to try to create some good in the midst of the hurt, so I decided to have a few widows over for a small dinner. We each shared memories of our hubbies along with a few tears. God comforts through people, and we experienced a sweet fellowship in our shared suffering.

I continued to enjoy His healing presence more and more, but was soon reminded that anything, from peanut butter in a jar to a familiar place, can blindside you and throw you backwards toward the pit. One dreary day in March, my chest began to hurt. I had been feeling a gripping pain for about a week and thought I just needed to relax. Due to the severity of the pain, I eventually called my daughter and told her that I was going to the ER to find out what was happening. Once I arrived, they did an EKG and my heart seemed good, so I was baffled as to why my body was behaving like this.

This was the first time I'd been back to the ER since Daryle had been there, and I kept praying that they wouldn't put me in Room 7, "Daryle's" room. I felt like I was suffocating, drowning in waves of memories. They thought I was crying because of the pain, but I was reliving that first horrible day of Daryle's diagnosis. I thought I would pass out from the stress. "God, help. Get me out of here." Unfortunately, I couldn't leave. Nausea and continued tightening in my chest prompted more EKGs, a stress test, and an endoscopy. They discovered that my vagus nerve was acting up. It is the longest of the cranial nerves, extending from the brainstem to the abdomen by way of multiple organs including the heart, esophagus, and lungs. Also known as cranial nerve X, the vagus forms part of the involuntary nervous system and commands unconscious body procedures, like keeping the heart rate constant and controlling food digestion. My body was having a problem managing both of these basics.

As bad as my physical condition was, I wanted to scream to everyone gathered around me that being in the ER and seeing Daryle's room, then being admitted, was stressing me out even more—that is, it was bad for my health. I prayed, "Dear God, please don't let them take me to the second floor—the cancer ward." They wheeled me up to the fifth floor past the CICU where Daryle had recovered from his brain surgery. I was sobbing, and the nurse asked me what she could do to ease my pain. I explained that it wasn't just the intense physical pain, but the excruciating pain of all the memories being dredged up from all that I'd been through in the last year.

At 3:30 a.m., I was awakened by another attack and they did another EKG. I was now wide awake. How could I possibly fall asleep covered with wires wrapped like vines around my body? I cried, "Lord, where are You? And PS I don't see any 'flowers' here." I turned on my side, draped one hand over the top of my raised bed, and asked God to "hold my hand" so that I could fall asleep. I drifted off. When I awoke a little later that morning, I opened to the "scripture of the day" on my phone. God showed me "flowers," but not as I expected. God has a sense of humor, "The grass withers and the flowers fall, but the Word of our God endures forever." (Isaiah 40:8, NIV) He knew I needed a laugh. Our little inside joke gave me an extra dose of comfort and joy in the midst of the chaos and gladdened my heart in the midst of the pain. He knew exactly where I was and why I was there and remained with me, as always.

The next day I got to go home and jumped back into my devotional, "Jesus Calling" by Sarah Young. That day read:

> "You are mine for all time—and beyond time, into eternity. No power can deny your inheritance in heaven. I want you to realize how utterly secure you are! Even if you falter as you journey through life, 'I will never *let go of your hand*!'"

Okay, wow! You really heard me, God!" Good meltdown. There are 365 days in this devotional. To be in the hospital talking to God about "flowers," asking Him to "hold my hand," and then seeing both of those things written in the devotionals for these specific days was reassurance that He was near, that He is a personal God, and that He intimately cared for me. He never stopped showing me how much He loved me.

I had believed in Him by faith for many years. I knew that God is Spirit and my spirit was connected to His Spirit, but I needed physical interaction, just like Adam, who got to walk with God. The Lord kept reaching down to me wherever I was, to demonstrate His love and presence. I believed before but once Daryle died, God was on the scene so many times, in so many ways that I could not deny it. I couldn't fabricate my own sense of calm and could never be comforted by "coincidence." God continually showed me in physical ways that He was with me and would help me and lead me through whatever lay ahead.

"The steps of good men are directed by the Lord. He delights in each step they take. If they fall, it isn't fatal, for the Lord holds them with His hand." (Psalm 37:23–24, TLB) "How good You are, oh my Jesus." Yes, not just "Jesus" but "my Jesus." I had never felt so close to the Lord in my life. Honestly, closeness takes two. Just like any relationship, it can't all be one-sided. I'm sure if all I ever did was ask my Daryle for things, we would have been in trouble, but we constantly shared our thoughts and feelings. God just wanted me to talk to Him about everything and not to hide anything. He wanted me to cry out to Him every single time I was weak, reminding me He was strong. If I was unsure, He was my assurance. He wanted me to depend on Him as my husband, my comforter, my counselor and friend.

Life ebbed and flowed. I had a promise from God, but I still struggled. God had clearly put His plan into motion. He wanted to bring His light into my life, and He did just that when David and Kathy returned in September of 2016. I said the same thing to the Lord as I had the last time. "If you have anything to say to me, I will hear it from David, Lord."

David was now eighty-one, so I jokingly asked him if he remembered what he had said to me before. He looked at me and said, "Of course I do."

"Oh, I was just wondering if you had anything else to say to me."

David got quiet, looked down, listening for the Lord to speak. He then looked at me and said, "Do you want an Englishman, Irishman, Scotsman, or German?"

"Umm, I hope you are talking about dogs!"

"No, Suzie, it's a man."

"What? Are you serious?"

He continued, "The Lord said it was not good for me to be alone."

Well, I agreed with that. I never wanted to be alone. I know some people don't mind it, maybe even enjoy it, but I would rather partner with someone.

Stephanie asked David, "Do you mean she has her pick of one of these four guys?"

"No" he simply said. "He's not from here."

Hmm, interesting. David's words catapulted me into a new way of thinking. I suddenly imagined a future unlike anything I'd considered over the last year and a half. I was still grieving but suddenly I thought, "Oh, my gosh! I have to exercise, ha ha. I've never been on a date with anyone but Daryle! What would that be like? What does he look like? Will he like me? And if he's not from here, where is he? Who is he?" I suddenly felt a happy buzz of excitement, believing that God had something amazing in store for me. But even I knew I wasn't ready, and laughingly asked God out loud, "Am I that much of a challenge that you can't find someone local and have to get someone from another state or country?"

My daughter replied, "No, Mummy, it's that you're that special."

Special? Or do you mean difficult? I had questions. Who could ever understand all that I'd been through, unless they'd been through it too? Who would be able to leave his family? How could that ever happen? Who would want to partner with me in my grief? I could not imagine any of it. I could not fathom someone coming alongside me as I was, but I did believe that God blesses "exceedingly and abundantly more than we can ever ask imagine or think," as His Word declares. So, I waited.

PART IV

A New Direction

CHAPTER 13

Beginning to Bloom

Widowhood tried to silence me. I wondered what causes a person to rise again when they are in the pit. For me, it was the constant pull of hope that His Word provided:

> "I took my troubles to the LORD; I cried out to him, and He answered my prayer."
>
> (Psalm 120:1, NLT)

> "Yes, my soul, find rest in God; my hope comes from Him."
>
> (Psalm 62:5, NIV)

> "Be glad for all God is planning for you. Be patient in trouble, and prayerful always."
>
> (Romans 12:12, TLB)

I asked Him to speak to me and He did. His Word was tangible CPR (cardio pulmonary resuscitation) reviving my heart. Every verse 'nto my soul. No one can administer CPR to them- ; to me, and to everyone around me, that I could 'e around me could save me. I was a mess. I had hread but God's Word is life, and the hope it ...eline. Hope was the lure. Hope was the rope that ...sed to pull me up out of the depth of my sorrow. He reached down to me, but I did have to take hold of the hope He offered, even though I may not have "felt" like it. My sorrow had been my world but I didn't want to live there anymore, and by an act of my conscious will I chose to grab on to what He offered. As He lifted me up, I would have to choose here and there, where to set my foot or rest my hand. He did the work but I chose to hang on. As He pulled I pushed up, as would a little toddler holding your hand as she learns to walk. Slowly, surely, hope led to hope, a word of promise led to a miracle and revelation about my future. I began to see Him and His hand move in my life as a widow.

I was shocked by the reality of God's Word and how concrete His involvement in my world had become. As insignificant as my needs may have been, God cared for me and responded to the cries of my heart. One of my favorite verses is in Psalms. "Because he bends down to listen, I will pray as long as I have breath!" (Psalm 116:2, NLT) When I first read this verse, it filled my heart with awe and gratitude. My heart attitude wasn't "gimme, gimme, gimme" but rather, "Wow, God, You want to listen to me? Who am I? I am nobody." But I came to realize, more than I ever had, that I was somebody to Him. His heart attitude toward me was all love, and I was stunned by the depth and sensitivity of His care.

There were so many instances where I imagined God tenderly bending, as a father does to a small child, to hear my little voice and my tearful pleas. He heard me. One day I happened to glance up at the peak of my roof (three stories up) and noticed a massive, buzzing hornets' nest. I asked my Heavenly Husband if He would please do what my earthly hubby would do and take care of this insurmountable (for me) problem. Later that day, I came home to find the hornets' nest on the ground. Really? The same day? Just hours later? I had not spoken to anyone but the Lord about this and just laughed out loud, "Thank you, God!" As it turns out, my son Rick "just happened" to notice the nest that day too (which had clearly been there for ages), climbed up onto the dangerous peak of the roof, and knocked it off!

I generally don't ask people for things. I ask Him. He knows who has the thing I need and hopefully they're listening to His prompting. One hot summer's day I stepped out onto my deck and exclaimed, "My Jesus. I love Your sun, but it's just too hot to stay out here to enjoy it." My simple prayer was, "I sure could use an awning." A few hours later, my friend Veronica called me and asked if I could help her organize a couple of rooms in her home, so off I went. As we were puttering about the house, I went to move a very large object and asked, "What in the world is this huge thing?"

Veronica didn't miss a beat and said, "It's an awning. Do you want it? It's brand new, but it just won't work where I needed. Now I'm stuck with it."

What? Are you kidding me? This was within a matter of hours and it's not like I begged God for an awning. I just talked to Him about everything as if He were my husband. I heard Veronica bellow to her sons, "Hey guys, go put this in Suzie's car." I giggled in disbelief all the way home. Every time I open it, I am reminded of God's incomprehensible graciousness to me. This is Who He is and what He does. He bends down and listens.

"Surely You have granted him unending blessings and made him glad with the joy of Your presence." (Psalm 21:6, NIV) So it has been with me. I began to trust (lean on, rely on, and press into) God for everything as never before. I had once been the can-do girl, but my sorrow had robbed me of that. Despite knowing that His Word said, "I can do all this through Him who gives me strength" (Philippians 4:13, NIV), I had become the "I just cannot do it" girl. But in Isaiah it says, "Behold, I am doing a new thing; now it springs forth, do you not perceive it?" I will make a way in the wilderness and rivers in the desert." (Isaiah 43:19, ESV) He was about to do new things that would set a course for my life that I never could have imagined.

I actually began to feel hope and wonder, things I had been afraid I wouldn't experience again. Looking back, I recognized that even in my deepest grief, I was privileged that the Lord had allowed me to be Daryle's wife, that we together declared, "As for me and my house we will serve the Lord." I had come far enough out of the fog to say, "Thank you, my Jesus, for it all." Because of everything God had asked me to walk through, not in spite of it all, I knew for sure that I would never walk alone. I knew that the One who held my hand could and did make good come from grief. I'd come to the point where I honestly committed out loud, "Whatever you ask me to do, God, I will do it. Seriously I will." I was finally convinced that He knew the bigger picture. He gave me glimpses of the future that He was orchestrating for me and I began to feel like I might like it, and like it without guilt. This is another part of a widow's walk. We sometimes feel survivor's guilt and don't allow ourselves to embrace life and the future.

I talked to Jesus about my future every morning. Each day I sat down with my coffee, my Bible, and my devotionals. On one particular day that I remember as clearly as if it were yesterday, I opened my Bible and ran across the scriptures that God had given Daryle two years before his death. Reading them again I was confused, because I had thought that these scriptures promised Daryle's healing. I asked God, "Did Daryle get it wrong?" I wondered if God got it wrong (which of course is ridiculous, but it still crossed my mind.) I couldn't understand where the breakdown had been. Suddenly, in prayer, on 2/18/17, God revealed the answer. The Lord showed me as I questioned number four that the first four scriptures He had given to Daryle were FOR Daryle and that the remaining five were for ME! I was shocked! It was as if a veil had been removed from my eyes.

Here is a second glance at them again with a little explanation:

1-4 FOR DARYLE

1. "I will sing and make music to the Lord." (Psalm 27:6, NIV)
   Daryle was a worship leader.
2. "Unless the Lord builds the house, the builders labor in vain." (Psalm 127:1)
   Strive as we may, only what the Lord builds lasts.
3. "Sing praises to God, sing praises; sing praises to our King, sing praises!" (Psalm 47:6, NLT)
   Daryle's life was a song of praise. He sang it to the Lord.
4. "The Lord sustains them on their sickbed and restores them from their bed of illness." (Psalm 41:3, NIV)
   Sustain: to keep alive; Restore: to bring back to oneself; Daryle was kept alive eight more months after the blood clots and God restored him back to himself in heaven.

5. "I will praise you, LORD, with all my heart; before the "gods" I will sing Your praise." (Psalm 138:1, NIV)
   I had declared God's praise on the radio, on YouTube videos, and in the first pages of this book.
6. "When I called, You answered me; You made me bold and stouthearted." (Psalm 138:3, NIV)
   Daryle was not either of these. Bold: Showing an ability to take risks, Stouthearted: fearless, spirited, spunky, intrepid, etc.
7. "The Lord will fulfill His purpose for me; Your steadfast love, O LORD, endures forever. Do not forsake the work of Your hands." (Psalm 138:8, ESV)
   God's purpose for me is His alone and I am in full agreement with it.
8. "Wait for the LORD; be strong and take heart and wait for the LORD." (Psalm 27:14, ESV)
   I waited, fainted, and waited for over four years to see the fulfillment of prophecy over me.
9. "They will still bear fruit in old age, they will stay fresh and green." (Psalm 92:14, NIV)
   I remember asking the Lord, "Wait—who are 'they'? Who will be of an old age? Me and my future husband?"

I was shocked and overcome as I realized that God had actually used Daryle to prophesy blessings into my future, one that he would never be able to share with me. God completely knows and ordains the beginning from the end.

I told God that I was never angry with Him about Daryle, but that in my feeble mind I was still trying to understand. "I thought You put us together forever." As I sat there in the quiet, the Lord spoke to my heart to reveal something else. "Suzie, I allowed Daryle to come home to propel you to the place I want you to be, to reach the 350 who do not know Me yet."

"Umm, Lord, I do not know 350 people."

His reply, "I do." Whether it was a literal 350 or that God would use a few to reach many, either in my lifetime, or after it, only He knew. Though I had no way to grasp then and don't completely understand now, I realized that God was declaring that there was a purpose in my loss, and that my suffering was going to be used to bless others.

"Lord, I guess I am selfish at heart. I want the one, my Daryle, and am not thinking of others. But now I can really see Your heart here. You truly want anyone who will say yes to You. You want to love on them the way You love on me." God has a way of humbling us with His love and deep compassion for the world and, in that moment, I cried out, "Jesus, may I be putty in Your hands. Use me!"

One week later an old friend called me trembling with excitement. I asked, "What's happened?"

She gasped, "Well, you won't believe it. I was approached by a radio station to do a talk show."

I responded, "Are you serious? What an honor! Wow! What a privilege! You can reach so many people that way. Good for you. I'm so happy for you."

"Good!" she said. "I am glad you think that, because I want you to be my cohost." She told me later that the Lord told her specifically that I was the only one to ask."

I blurted, "Happiness has left the building! That's the last thing in the world I want to do right now! Are you crazy? The only thing I know about the radio is turning it on and off!"

Before I finished my sentence, the Lord spoke to my heart, "Remember, Suzie? You said if I asked…."

Ugh! "Okay, Lord, but I think You are making a big mistake!"

I agreed to do it. I could hear my Daryle saying, "Honey! Man radio!" That's what I called his radio talk shows because on the programs he listened to, men went on and on and on about sports. Ha! God has a funny sense of humor. I know Daryle would just be so proud. Good grief, radio!

The Lord knows what He is doing, and I was in awe of the things unfolding right in front of my eyes. Could this be the ministry that was mentioned by Deb just weeks after Daryle died? I was now coanchoring on an uplifting Christian talk show where we interviewed authors, business owners, and everyday folks who had tragedy to triumph testimonies. I also did a segment solely for widows at the end of each show. It was aired out of Boston on WROL. Only God knew how much I would enjoy this! My life changed overnight, like there was a cosmic finger snap and puff, I woke up in front of a microphone with headphones on.

This assignment lasted a year and, literally the week that it ended, my son encouraged me to start a video blog. Once again, my response was, "What? Are you nuts? I am not going in front of a camera. That is *NEVER* going to happen! It was bad enough that I had to talk on the radio, but at least they couldn't see me!" There was no way I was going to put myself in this vulnerable position. But God relentlessly worked through my son. Rick actually took me by the shoulders, turned me around, and walked me to the computer, saying, "Let's just do a practice run. We won't air it. Just see how it goes."

God is so funny. I looked over at my son and a dear family friend who had joined us and asked, "How was that?" The tears in their eyes spoke volumes. Rick convinced me to air it later that day and so began Episode 1 of "Widows' Wednesday." Good grief, YouTube! I could not conceive of the impact that this single act of reluctant obedience would have on my life and the lives of others. I had no idea that God was going to create a lifetime of love and friendships with women all over the globe.

God was constantly looking after me and fulfilling His plans and purposes. I felt like a nobody, unable to do the tasks He set before me, but His word says, "May He equip you with all you need for doing His will." (Hebrews 13:21, NLT) Even when I would dig my heels in, He was long suffering toward me, and gently eased me forward through kind and powerful words from others or irresistible invitations. The words spoken over me were all coming to pass. God knew how much I would hurt in this painful season of my life, but He also knew I would heal… that HE would heal me, and that He would be with me as husband, father, friend, provider, and comforter. My faith kept growing. I was astounded by how many things God did to prove His presence to me.

He continued to respond to the simplest desires of my heart, things that no one else knew. One day as I sat at a friend's house, I thought about how much I would enjoy chicken thighs for dinner. Moments later, I got a call from my mom, saying chicken thighs were "Buy One, Get One Free," and that she'd put a package in my freezer! I would realize my gas tank was low, and random people would hand me cash to pay for gas or whatever I needed. I personally experienced the truth of His word, "He defends the cause of the fatherless and the widow, and loves the foreigner residing among you, giving them food and clothing." (Deuteronomy 10:18, NIV)

Widows face so many challenges. Finances and provision are

often at the top of the list. Jesus says He is our husband, and I was getting a lot of practice learning to depend on Him in a literal way in that role. As I prayed about my finances, I had a dream. I went to heaven. I saw Jesus. He was standing in front of what looked like a communion table, but it was made of gold. There were some items on the top of it that I didn't recognize, also made of gold. Jesus had a beautiful smile on His face and His beautiful eyes were locked on me. He was wearing an apron full of what looked like pounds of butter. He held the bottom corners of it as He rolled it forward towards me. I remember thinking, "What is this?" I watched the "butter" fall to the ground. As they dropped, I bent to pick them up for Him (as if Jesus needed my help) but realized as I did that these were not sticks of butter at all but were actually bars of gold. I woke up. My first thought was that God had shown me that "provision" was coming my way. Either that or I was going to get a lot of butter!

Right after the dream, my birthday rolled around again just as I faced off against another widow battle: rebellious appliances! My stove was leaking gas and it was determined that I needed a new one ASAP! As I was praying, I said, "Lord, you know my situation and, well, would You please take care of the stove for me?" A couple of days later my mom mentioned to me that Sears had some stoves on a one-day sale. I could get a brand-new stove for less than half of the original price!

"Okay, Mom. Just pick it out for me. I will be in Boston today and can't do it."

Well Mom had coupons and I had birthday money from family, so I essentially paid nothing out of pocket for my brand- new stove!

Even in the midst of God's Presence, we can grow physically and emotionally weary. One particularly hectic day I had worked for a friend from early morning until late at night. I was exhausted. I wanted some comfort and to know in some tangible way that He was with me. I wanted a shout out from my heavenly husband, since my earthly husband was gone. I missed the simple, "Hey, how are you doing, honey? I'm here. How was your day?" So I said to my Jesus, "Lord, I haven't seen any flowers lately. I would love some flowers by midnight tonight." On the way home I stopped at IKEA, where they had a display of pink and white peonies on sale. They were beautiful and cheap, so I bought them. My mother had just given me two decorative mason jars that very morning, so I popped the white ones in a jar downstairs and the pink ones next to my bed. As I laid my head on the pillow, I glanced at my clock. It was 15 minutes before midnight. The Lord gently spoke to my heart, "Do you like your flowers?" I giggled out loud. I never even realized that this was His provision. He had given me the flowers I'd asked for. As if that weren't enough, I turned on KLOVE in the morning, a local Christian radio station. I learned that it was National Flower Day, a celebration I never even realized existed. I could feel my Lord winking at me, as if He had dedicated the entire day to me. To someone else, National Flower Day would have meant nothing, but to me it felt like a giant hug all day long.

He shows up in so many unexpected ways, and His ways aren't always our way, but we can trust Him. I know it's difficult to trust someone you can't see. That is faith. I don't see the wind but I feel it. I don't see electricity but I know when it's working. And so it is with God. I sometimes just sit quietly and ask the Lord to let me feel His presence, and a sense of liquid love and calming peace just pours over me. I can't make myself feel that type of peace. I know it's not something I have within me or can conjure up with breathing exercises and meditation. I have felt His tangible presence so often at this point, I simply know and trust. There's a bumper sticker "No Jesus, No peace. Know Jesus, Know Peace!" This is the simple truth... the truth this world needs in order to find the true peace it craves. This truth and His peace sustained me through all that He walked me through.

Even with His peace, life can be frustrating when things seem to spiral out of control. Trouble may just keep coming at you like rhythmic waves pushing you under until you feel like you are drowning. I pondered the purpose of waves. The funny thing about waves is that they are also a powerful force to carry us forward. The definition of a wave is: "a disturbance on the surface, a surging or progressive movement, a swell, a rush." A deep underwater wave is caused by an earthquake which may cause a tsunami and, with it, great destruction; for example, our spouses' deaths.

I was trying to fall asleep one night and, as I finally drifted off, God startled me awake, whispering, "There is no surfer without the wave." My eyes popped open as I wondered what He could have meant by that. I immediately researched waves and learned that the surfer is the one who rides the wave; and not only rides it, but rides it standing up. He is on top of it. He is the overcomer. He climbs onto the board, his foundation, which is tethered to him. He makes sure that he has firm footing before he tries to ride the wave. Jesus is our firm foundation and we are safe in Him. There still is no promise that we won't tumble, get seaweed in our eyes, saltwater up our noses, and sand in our ears. We may get tossed and hurt, but most surfers get right back up to ride again. That needs to be us. I was encouraged by this simple illustration, having ridden the wave of tragedy for so long. In the beginning, however, all I knew was the wreckage of the tsunami. I also knew from observation and experience that the ocean is rarely calm, and that waves inevitably come again.

One Saturday I spiked a fever of 103 and was quite sick. Mom had come over with some homemade soup and finally got me out of bed. As we sat there, my mom asked me about a few pages of memories and miracles that I'd written down in the months after Daryle's death. I told her that she was welcome to read them as I sipped her soup. She sat right down at my computer and excitedly began reading. Now I felt sick for a different reason. Gosh, I thought, "It's weird for someone, even your own mom, to read the secret thoughts of your heart." But as she finished, Mom smiled with tears in her eyes and said, "You've captivated me, and I want to read more. You've got to finish your story."

"Really, Mom? If the Holy Spirit wants me to write a book, then the Holy Spirit would have to tell me to do it Himself. No offense to the Lord, but considering the pain involved, I can't do it."

My fever broke and the next day, I went to church. My friend Nicole said, "Oh, I need to speak with you—don't let me forget." I went up for prayer, and she prayed for me and related this story to me. Her friend's husband had just died. Nicole told her newly widowed friend how God had been my husband, and He would be hers as well. Having fallen on very hard times and now relying on local assistance for meals, this woman skeptically said to God, "All I really want right now are three cans of creamed corn." After rifling through eight boxes of cans at the soup kitchen, the only thing this woman found in the ninth and last box were exactly three cans of creamed corn. "It worked!" she shouted. It's not that God is a vending machine, but He makes special provision and promises for widows, and she exercised a mustard seed of faith and was astounded by God's faithfulness. Oh my goodness, what joy that brought to my heart as I thought, "My Jesus,

You are there for her too." She didn't need the three cans of corn as much as she needed to know God was with her in her hardship.

As I turned to walk away, Nicole went on to say, "Oh, by the way, the Holy Spirit has been pressing me all week to tell you to finish your book."

I spun around and asked, "What did you say?" Unreal. God was already speaking to someone else (Nicole) about my future, my writing, and His desire for me, before I even became sick and before that pivotal conversation with my Mom.

Then, the following week, our pastor mentioned in his sermon, "For example, if God wants you to write a book, do it." My family immediately spun around in unison and looked at me.

"Okay, Lord, I get it, I get it... I know, I know. I said I would do whatever you asked."

I was so curious about what He wanted to do in my life and began to realize that He had a specific plan for me that involved writing my testimony. Think again about this scripture: "Now all glory to God, who is able, through His mighty power at work within us, to accomplish infinitely more than we might ask or think." (Ephesians 3:20, NLT) You know when I thought back to the K-cup coffee, God hadn't just met my need. He exceeded my need! I knew He wanted to bless me and bring others to the genuine knowledge of Himself, so that they might experience what I had... His absolute and unconditional love. It made me think of the Biblical account of the wedding at Cana in Galilee. The hosts had run out of wine, so Mary (Jesus' mother) asked Jesus to provide for them. He had not yet revealed Himself to those around Him, so Mary simply said to the servants, "Do whatever He tells you to do." These are the last recorded words of Mary. "Do what He tells you to do": instruction for life. Jesus told them to fill six

20–30-gallon stone pots to the brim with water, and he transformed the water into wine. In today's economy, that's about 228 bottles or roughly $4,500 worth of top-quality wine. What an amazing representation of the ordinary life without Jesus versus abundant life with Him. Even now, His graciousness to those who believe and to those who don't overwhelms me.

His loving kindness makes me cry, "Lord, I appreciate You for who You are and all You do for me. I sit and look out my window in the morning and look around at nature and I realize that none of this would be here if not for You setting it in place." When I see the sky, the trees, the oceans, I thank Him for them. I know my place. I could never create such beauty and know that this kind of power does not dwell within me. How wonderful it is that the One who does have that power wants an intimate relationship with me, and with all of us. As I gaze up at the stars, His beautiful creation speaks to me. "When I consider Your heavens, the work of Your fingers, the moon and the stars, which You have set in place, what is mankind that You are mindful of them, human beings, that You care for them?" (Psalm 8:3–4, NIV)

CHAPTER 14

"H2"

If the Lord can set the stars in heaven, I guess appointing the details of my life is not a challenge for Him, especially if I don't get in the way. God was actively working. I could see it. I could feel it. I'd been told. I began to feel like I should kick it up a notch and actively "work" too, so I intentionally began to pray for my future husband, God's purpose, and my desires. God had called me "bold," so I was going boldly to the throne of grace with something I hadn't really talked about out loud... love and a husband. Though others had spoken words over me concerning a husband, I hadn't really allowed myself to consider it, but now as healing and hope increased, I felt I had permission to love again and declared, "God, I am all in!"

This was my prayer: "Lord, I know You know exactly who this man is and where he lives. You know his name. I know none of this, so I'm going to give him a name, "H2" for Hubby Number Two." God used the nickname "H2" to reveal things to me and to motivate me. I love that He spoke my language and met me where I was. One day, I pulled into Dunkin Donuts and saw a Humvee. On the back panel of the car was an "H2" chrome emblem. I immediately felt the burden to pray for my future husband, specifically for the events and decisions facing him. I began to share my hope for a husband with others.

Every year for the first two weeks of January, our church fasts and prays for many different things. On one of those nights, my friend Elda verbally proclaimed that she was believing God for a husband by the end of 2017! I glanced over at her and gave her the thumbs up. This is a subject that we had discussed in great detail. Her confidence encouraged me to do the same. I divulged to the Lord and everyone else present that I was going to ride her skirt tails and ask for the same thing! I felt like a fuel tank in me burst open. My faith ignited. I experienced the opening of a new world, new hope, and new expectations.

Part of me knew that bringing a man into my life would change my everyday routine, might interrupt my quiet times, and certainly would alter the order that was slowly returning to my life. I began to imagine what it would be like to NOT be a widow anymore. I had lived in this place for over four years. The thought of leaving this familiar territory was unnerving. Throughout my widowhood, I had been completely under God's care. But now I felt like my "Father" was about to give me away. He had taught me a lot during my intimate season with Him, and these things now came to feel like parting gifts, such as:

1. If you allow the Lord to do what He wants, He is going to bring out every beautiful thing He has planted in you while you walk in the desert.
2. Widowhood provides a chance to be alone with God, and to simply *be* God's, no one else's. My spirit loved this, even though my heart was lonely for human companionship.
3. Lastly, death provides perspective. Things that seem essential

> become unimportant. Things that are troublesome become endearing. What we worry about and what we value can dramatically change.

In the weeks and months that followed, I began to experience a quickening in my spirit, an even more activated sense of excitement and anticipation. Many times I went to the altar concerning H2. One Sunday, a dear member of the prayer team prayed over me. Suddenly she said, "One word keeps coming to me … rebirth. Something is about to be born into your life that God has called 'showers of blessings' for you." I was excited. I knew that my heart's desire would be coming soon. My knowing was solid. That's what faith is: "Now faith is the substance of things hoped for, the evidence of things not yet seen." (Hebrews 11:1, NKJV) My H2 was on the way! Oh, my goodness. What would he be like? How will I meet him? How will he understand the depths of my pain? Will he be funny? I'd made a list of all that I hoped for in my H2. "Funny" was definitely number one on my list!

Decades before, Daryle and I were just kids and we each made a list of what we wanted in a mate, not knowing that the other had done the same. After discovering his, I mentioned that I got everything on my list but one thing.

"What was that?" Daryle asked.

"An accent," I said.

So how interesting would it be that the one thing I didn't get on my original list could possibly happen now? David had asked me if I wanted an Englishman, Irishman, Scotsman, or German. Having received a word like that, my brain now went into overdrive wondering everywhere I looked, "Is it him? Is it him? Dear Lord, please not him! He's too young, or nope, he is way too old." H2 or no H2, I continued to wait on the One who had been my faithful husband, as He promised.

One afternoon in February 2017, my friend Veronica called. We had been widowed around the same time. She had been deep in prayer when she felt the Lord give her a Word for both of us. This is what she shared:

> "I speak My peace on you. I am the Lord your God. I want to make clear to you and Suzie that your husbands did not die due to sin. I had planned the length of their lives from the beginning of time. I knew the days. I had a different plan for you all along. My plan was for your husbands to be stepping stones in your lives. I had in mind for you to marry twice all along. I wanted your first husband to lay a foundation for your second husband to fulfill. The blessings I have for the two of you is to receive your husbands. My sons in whom I am well pleased will enter your lives soon. The blessings I have for you are more than you can comprehend. The lives the two of you will live are different than you will imagine. The blessing I have for the two of you are that your husbands will be the fulfillment of the plans I have for you. They will bless you to accomplish the will of your Father in Heaven."

Soon after, I was praying for my husband to be and said, "Lord, I know you are working on bringing H2 my way. I just wanted to say I trust You and if he is to be my 'hubby to be,' I'm ready."

An hour later, I went to my friend Jan's house. I idled at the bottom of her driveway getting ready to pull out when I noticed a green car coming. I had to watch and wait for it to pass, so as it went by, I glanced at the license plate which to my astonishment was H2B! I could have searched forever and would never have found that, nor have I seen it since! You could have knocked me over with a feather! A feeling of utter dependence, as if I were an infant, came over me. I felt utterly surrendered to God. This simple encounter proved to me, if to no one else, that God was working on it! I loved how the Lord shared these personal hints and nudges of encouragement with me in tiny increments, so as not to overwhelm me. He was coming. I knew it. I didn't want to miss it, but had God presented me with a full-blown husband all at once at that moment in time, I am pretty sure I would have had a meltdown!

As I waited on the Lord, I received wonderful news from my daughter that I was going to be a grandmother again come Christmastime. I had so much to look forward to. In the meantime, I was quite active working with widows via online widows groups, connecting with ladies through emails and meetings. In my prayer time on April 6, 2017, I said to the Lord, "My Jesus, I know how You have helped me. As Your word says, You have been my husband. But Lord, I'm curious: how do You help the man since Your word does not say that You will be his wife?" I decided (in hindsight it was God's leading) to go to the online widows' groups that I was working with and ask some of the men if they would share how God had helped them through widowerhood. To my surprise, most of them answered with "Hello, beautiful…." So I did the only thing I could do: I deleted them! This was harder than I thought. There must be one guy out there who will honestly answer my question. I actually said to myself I am going to field this for exactly two days tops and then I'm out! So the very next day, April 7, 2017, I received a response from a man named Bruce LaRue who said; "What a beautiful (almost deleted him right then) mission statement to help ease the pain of widows." Wow! Well, that was different. Mission statement?

The only way he would know I even had a mission statement was if he checked out my Facebook profile which is linked to my widows group. I thought that was a wise way to get to know more about me and thought I should do the same before we spoke. As I clicked on his Facebook page, I started to see the people in his world: his daughter, son, and other family members, including his wife who I realized had also died from brain cancer. Suddenly I came upon words his wife had posted that clearly came from the depth of her heart:

> "***TODAY I FEEL COMPELLED TO TELL ALL MY FAITHFUL PRAYER PARTNERS A SPECIAL THANK YOU FOR ALL YOUR LOVE AND SUPPORT. Most especially, I need to share my heart for my dear Bruce***. There are no words to express what an AMAZING and LOVING care giver my dear husband is in the middle of some extremely stressful and often painful circumstances. Please continue to pray for his physical and mental strength. We both know my prognosis isn't what we'd want it to be. Faced with our reality, Bruce has become my Superman. In addition to working his crazy swing shift job, he is still finding time to take care of the house and all that it requires. His care for me is angelic. He somehow knows what I need before I even ask. We've lived a beautiful life together and even in the midst of this ugly disease, my dear husband continues to love me as if I were his sweet young bride. God has blessed us with the assurance that He has fulfilled His promise and we are indeed one. No earthly circumstance will ever separate us, and we know we will have an eternity to walk

hand-in-hand. Thank you, Jesus, for this—one of your most precious gifts, GOD—YOU ARE SO GOOD!!!!"

I wondered who could know him better than his wife. In an instant, I was given a glimpse into his true character and I was amazed. I quickly responded with all sincerity that I would love to hear his story. I'd heard from his wife in her own words and felt reassured about talking to him. I had my nephew's birthday party that day and responded that I would be back online around three—"ish." He asked if he could call instead. I thought, "UMMM, sure. Um, why would he call me? What would I say?" This felt weird. I was unnaturally nervous. At 3:05 p.m., I received a text asking, "Is it 'ish' yet?" I thought, "Hilarious!" Sure.

This is his story.

CHAPTER 15

The Other Side

MY HEART WENT ON A JOURNEY,

Led by the Holy One,
As if I were a rainbow,
Searching for the sun.

Just like the sunny day,
That turns into a storm,
The clouds began to gather,
The winds began to warn.

And at that very moment,
The rain began to fall,
The thunder terrified us,
We thought we lost it all.

But don't you trust Me Peter?
What about you John?
That storm is just a picture,
Of what you'll overcome.

The clouds began to part,
The Father showed His face,
In the image of the rainbow,
To remind us of HIS grace!

~BRUCE LARUE

God has always been there, protecting and watching over me. Raised in an alcoholic household, my earthly father only spoke the name Jesus Christ as a curse word. I told my mother that I did not believe in God because if there were a god, how could all this bad stuff happen in our home? But then a high school friend and faithful follower of Jesus encouraged me to go to a Young Life meeting. I loved the meetings, but still did not understand the reality of God until a weekend trip in the autumn of 1973. After a week of hearing the Gospel, I was encouraged to go out to find a quiet place to talk to God. I sat under a tree in the brisk night air looking at the star-filled sky. The question in my heart was simple: "Do you believe that everything you see could have happened by chance, or do you believe I created it?" I knew He was real at that moment, and accepted Jesus as my LORD and Savior that night. Little did I comprehend the change I was about to experience.

The next morning, I woke up with the most extraordinary sense of life and vivid joy that I'd ever had. It was as if those millions of stars that I gazed at the night before were permanently attached to my soul.

The countenance of my entire being was lifted beyond anything that I could have imagined or generated on my own. I had an inexplicable encounter with the God of the universe and I knew it. I experienced an irrational, supernatural hope that was not contingent on anything I could see, touch, or create, but my joy was overflowing beyond my ability to contain it. No one in my presence was safe from the overflow. If you were near me, you were going to be saturated with joy. Every time I called on God following this encounter, God touched me with His presence and I literally felt it physically. This testified to Him and confirmed my initial experience. The first thing He told me to do was read the Bible and at seventeen, I lay on my bed and read it cover to cover. Words from Romans jumped off the page and came to life, imbedding themselves in my heart, "For I am persuaded that neither death nor life, nor angels nor principalities nor powers, nor things present nor things to come, nor height nor depth, nor any other created thing, shall be able to separate us from the love of God which is in Christ Jesus our Lord." (Romans 8:38–39, NKJV) That verse was to become especially important to me. I knew God was real, but I would come to learn that there is also an enemy of our souls who was real too.

My extreme joy lasted for a season, but I was not discipled and taught about the deeper things of God: Who He was, and how I was to live? I lived in an immoral world and was susceptible to the influences of that world. My choices and my way of thinking kept me from advancing the way I might have. I wanted to be accepted by my peers as did most teenagers and began hanging out with friends in bars and dance clubs. In the parable of the sower it says of the seed, "Some fell on the rocky places, where it did not have much soil. It sprang up quickly, because the soil was shallow. But when the sun came up, the plants were scorched, and they withered because they had no root." (Mark 4:5–6, NIV) So began my downward spiral. Little by little, compromise by compromise, my walk with God faltered.

I knew nothing of the "Christian Walk" growing up. Living with a violent, unreliable father provided no earthly role model for Godly behavior. Fathers need to teach their sons how to be men, but all he taught me was what I did not want to be. There was no physical or emotional affection. There was absolutely no example of relationship. As a young man I had few meaningful lasting bonds with others. Consequently I was reluctant to marry because I was afraid. All I had seen was heartache. Despite my deep apprehension and my many missteps, God was still with me and, in 1977, He sent me a treasure named Diane. He brought this lovely young woman all the way from Indiana to my back door in West Virginia, and I fell in love. Even so, I wasn't sure what God wanted for me. I told the LORD that I could not marry unless I audibly heard His voice. I soon heard His voice telling me that He had given me a "gift." God says, "He who finds a wife finds a good thing and obtains favor from the Lord." (Proverbs 18:22, ESV) I felt that the Lord was not pleased that I did not have the courage to accept His gift and to act on what He had placed in my heart. But His love and grace for me was sufficient to cover my doubts. Thankfully, God was speaking to Diane as He spoke to me, telling her that He was pleased with her for accepting His call to marry me. He further promised that once married she would not be barren, as doctors had told her.

We married in August of 1978. God immediately used Diane to bless me in so many ways. I suddenly had a helper and someone who saw potential in me that I had not recognized. Her strong moral code propelled me toward God and doing things His way. Life changed for the better. My son Benjamin was born in January of 1981. By spring of that same year, we decided to move back to Evansville, Indiana, Diane's home town. Another gift was the birth of my daughter Megan on Valentine's Day, 1988. There were profound moments of joy as we grew as a family. We experienced growing prosperity, going from living in my mother-in-law's basement to renting a house, to buying a home. We also enjoyed the everyday: vacations, baseball games, basketball coaching, and dance lessons. Our life was a little slice of the American dream nestled in the Midwest.

Moving back to Indiana in the 1980s jump-started my spiritual growth as well. This was a time of happiness and peace, but by the mid-1990s, Diane began to have serious physical problems. By the mid-2000s she was disabled. Her life—that is, our life—became one filled with surgeries and illnesses. Diane and I were hard workers, and God prospered us in Indiana. But despite our successes, personal determination and faith, life became much more difficult. I came to feel like the wind was always blowing against me. Diane faced constant physical trials and my children faced severe challenges of their own.

Life was no longer the fairy tale I'd expected. In the midst of our troubles, I continued to work very hard. At this stage, I would have been very grateful for encouragement from anywhere, but even in my professional life I did not receive the expected promotion, even when my performance was acknowledged as exemplary in comparison to my peers. When a man works hard, achieves results, and exceeds corporate expectations, he expects to be rewarded. Man failed me. God did not. He used this opportunity to prove that He was my faithful Father. Every time one assignment ended, He opened another door that was even better than the one before. Many of these jobs were humbling. They consisted of off shift, or rotating shift, work that others might refuse. I didn't realize it at the time, but God was cultivating perseverance in me to prepare me for what lay ahead.

Diane lived in constant pain. Everything is difficult when a person you care about hurts continually. I remember once during an especially hard time I was praying (or actually complaining) to God about my circumstances. Instead of the comforting response I expected, the Lord told me that my wife would die. Although it would be years before this would come to pass, I never shared this with another living soul. This might seem like a horrible prophesy, but in retrospect these were loving words which gave me peace as Diane's illnesses progressed. It was a gift that revealed God's plans and purposes. I then knew that my mission was to pray for her, comfort her, minister to her, and to love her until her last breath on earth and, more importantly, to glorify God in her suffering. I knew I was not responsible to save her. That was His job. "Why, even the hairs of your head are numbered" (Luke 12:7, ESV), and the days of her life as it says in Psalms: "You saw me before I was born. Every day of my life was recorded in your book. Every moment was laid out before a single day had passed." (Psalm 139:16, NLT)

Diane suffered through a series of horrific problems. During one of her back surgeries, she contracted a hospital infection called MRSA. It attacks the immune system and the internal organs, wreaking havoc in the body. It can and did manifest itself through many different illnesses. This infection resulted in blood poisoning which required emergency surgery to clean the wound out. She was then given an antibiotic which she was allergic to. It caused a horrendous rash that covered her entire body.

Despite the agony, disorientation, and confusion, she maintained a sense of hope and a sense of humor. One day she went to bed, saying,

"I'm not waking up tomorrow morning!" The morning came and she was wide awake. I led her to the white-tiled bathroom and she asked, "Is this Heaven?"

"No, honey," I replied. "It's just a bathroom."

"Good," she said. "It looks like a bathroom."

When the one you're caring for cracks a joke, it eases the reality of what you're really facing. Her dignity and her strength in the midst of her suffering witnessed to everyone around her.

Fast forward to September of 2011. Diane began to have migraines. She suffered from late September through November with acute headaches. One day while I was at work, Diane drove to our local Walmart. After shopping, she got back in her car and had no idea where she was or how to get home. She said she didn't know what to do, so she started following a random car. While driving, she swerved over the center line and caused a minor accident. She was then taken to the police department where she was treated very harshly.

Believing she was under the influence, they sent her to the hospital for a drug test.

We believed, however, that her disorientation might be due to negative drug interactions, resulting from the amount of medication she was on. We found none but, after this incident, it became my job to monitor the intake of her meds. This was demeaning to a capable, self-aware woman who knew she had done nothing wrong. By early November, after the fourth round of migraine medicine, our local pharmacist wisely recommended that we look for the cause of her headaches rather than simply treating her symptoms. On Friday, November 11, 2011, I took Diane to the emergency room because her pain had become so severe and relentless and the medication wasn't touching it. Tests and scans revealed the shocking cause of her trouble.

She had a large mass on the right side of her brain which pathology diagnosed as glioblastoma multiform (GBM). This is "the most aggressive form of brain cancer." We were told that she had stage 4, and her life expectancy was less than a year. It was a medical fact that there was no cure, thus they called this cancer the "Terminator."

We were all stunned. After all we had been through, now this? When things get tough, God often sends people like a flood. Megan decided to move home to help care for her mom and to share whatever time remained. Her sisters, LaDonne and Connie, were also always available to do whatever was needed despite the fact that they lived some distance away and had families of their own. I so appreciated their loving care for Diane. Week after week, month after month, these strong women were there for us.

They weren't the only blessing. Prior to Diane's diagnosis, she had been in such pain that her pain doctor had done a complete examination and reviewed all of her medication for negative interactions. We found nothing at the time, but as soon as we got Dianne's cancer diagnosis, I went back to him and shared our report. Unknown to me at the time, he was a minister. He asked to come to our house to pray for Diane and me. In a private moment during his visit, he asked me what I wanted. I answered, "I want what God wants, and I want to care for her in a way that will glorify Him."

He told me, "It won't be easy. Sometimes God allows things to take a person more quickly rather than to allow them to suffer."

I accepted that, knowing "the secret things belong to the Lord our God, but the things revealed belong to us and our children forever." (Deuteronomy 29:29, ESV) Her appointed time was in His hands. Oh, how little we understand of the tender mercies of our loving God. I was about to witness His goodness in the midst of our trials.

The next seven months were filled with decisions about treatment and the agony of "what ifs." In the presence of pain and uncertainty, the beauty of love, friends, and family support became so much more evident. Life became more precious. Diane and I reflected constantly on the reality expressed in the Bible "For man does not know his time." (Ecclesiastes 9:12, ESV) We were struck by the limited time man is given to live out life on planet earth. Diane even sighed one day, "Fifty-five years ... this is all I get?" At the same time, she said she was not afraid to die. Diane truly achieved a sense of spiritual balance and understanding. Her faith could not be shaken despite everything she would have to endure. We walked through the pain, the deep, deep pain of the soul that only people who travel this path understand.

Her reality made us both hypersensitive to the gifts that surrounded us every day. We experienced healing in personal relationships as we focused on what was important and what was not. Family and a lifetime of friends all rallied and prayed against the "odds." We had hope, but God had privately given me foreknowledge (which I never shared with Diane) that this was to be the end of her days on earth. Ironically, that word brought peace in this most difficult trial. Together, we both understood that God's certain goal is to get HIS children home to heaven. He had made a glorious way for all of us to do that. He sent Jesus—the way, the truth, and the life. God's word says, "I have said these things to you, that in me you may have peace. In the world you will have tribulation. But take heart; I have overcome the world." (John 16:33, ESV) Knowing that trials are part of every human life and that our circumstances were common to man, we entrusted ourselves to His care. In retrospect, I believe wholeheartedly that this brain cancer mercifully shortened the suffering of my Diane.

Diane was diagnosed on 11-11-11. God is in every detail of our lives. When I realized the date, I looked up the number 11 in Biblical Numerology. It is described as representing "imperfection, disorder, disintegration, dis-organization, and chaos." Surely this was the unfortunate condition of my love's body. The tumor continued to grow, even though the radiation treatment was intended to shrink it. Knowing that man's way wasn't working, I cried out to God as she suffered. Twice in my life I have felt a profound depth of need. Once in my youth when I begged my heavenly Father to send her, and again as I begged my Father to let her enter His paradise. I prayed,

"She cries for You Lord.
She cries for needs that I am unable to attend.
Please have mercy Lord of all,
in honor of the shelter that she has been for so many.
But in our suffering, glorify Yourself
as it should be for the sake of others
who may need to see Your glory,
and give us the strength to endure."

Nine days later, after only seven months receiving the highest level of radiation allowed by law, she passed in her sleep. Only fifty-five years were given to Charlotte Diane LaRue, but she accomplished her mission. Her faith, strength, and obedience to her divine calling on my life rescued me and put me on a more fruitful path. God does that in marriage. Even when it's hard, he uses our spouses to transform us and purify us. That transformation continued after Diane was gone. I distinctly remember going home one evening for a shower and a little rest. As I put my hand on the doorknob, the realization struck me that my Diane would never again enter this house … the house that we had dreamed of and built together. Uncertainty crept in. What do I do now? How do I live? There was nowhere to go and no one to whom I could go without crushing them with the weight of my sorrow.

The following days were filled with such deep grief. As a man, I simply wanted to be alone in my grief. I considered walking the Appalachian Trail alone or buying a new car and a little camper and escaping to the wilds. Losing Diane caused me to cry from a depth that I never knew existed. I cried not only for the loss of my life's partner for over thirty-three years, but also for how painful our last years together had been, and for all that I never would have with her. We dream. Maybe our dreams are fairy tales. I had dreamed of happily ever after and growing old together, but this didn't look like that at all. I was sad and bewildered by how cruel life could be even in the midst of God's Presence and tender mercies. He does not say He will spare us from trials, but promises "And the Lord, He is the One who goes before you. He will be with you, He will not leave you nor forsake you; do not fear no be dismayed." (Deuteronomy 31:8, NKJV)

The following weeks and months were filled with visits from well-wishers, and family and friends who just wanted to check up on me to make sure I was okay. Despite the love people showed me, the void remained. I realized more than ever before that a wife is the heart of the home. This encompasses so much ... gathering for meals, decorating for holidays, celebrating events, organizing baby pictures, preserving family history. Her absence left a hole that no one could fill, but when the Lord sustains life, as He did mine, He has a purpose for that life. I knew I had to keep moving forward into that purpose, though I had no idea what that would look like.

I was just trying to gather myself back up again. The irony is that you have to leave your former life behind even as you have to bring some of it forward with you. Deciding exactly what goes and what stays is painful. I recognized right away that removing Diane's clothes was important to help me begin again. Diane's nieces took on that task. The most difficult thing I had to do was to go through her personal things. For example, I seldom ventured into her purse during our thirty-three years of marriage. Touching something that personal, that she had touched every day for decades, resurrected my acute grief. Occupying space that had once been hers was also difficult for me. I could only sleep on a sliver of the bed. My home was filled with memories of Diane, but God had released me from the burden of care and the labor of love so that I could begin to seek His unfolding plan and purpose for me.

I was now free to work the demanding 12-hour rotating shift job that had been such a challenge during her prolonged illnesses. I hoped to work until I was sixty, then hoped to enjoy early retirement. In the meantime, I was trying to find my "new normal." I had been so focused on my Diane, but suddenly had the opportunity to engage with others. I reached out to family and they reached out to me.

Within a few months, my son invited me to a weekend retreat with him called "Walk to Emmaus." Because I had the time off from work and could not for the life of me think of a reason to refuse him, I told him I would attend. Ben acted as the music director for the weekend, so I thought my involvement would give us some quality time together. The challenge for me was that I had relished my isolation. This weekend consisted of lots of concentrated focus studies in small groups that required a lot of personal interaction. Though I dutifully participated, I wasn't really ready for that. Unfortunately I was still grieving and retreated back to my room during breaks where I sobbed inconsolably. I think they heard me!

Interacting with others wasn't the only challenge I faced. This was a beautiful weekend that had been bathed in prayer by hundreds and hundreds of dedicated people whose only purpose was to serve and show us the love of God. One of the ways they blessed us was with food. All weekend I had tried to avoid the table with the snacks and sweets on it because I had lost a little weight and was trying to maintain a healthier diet. I had done so well that I felt I earned just one little treat.

Toward the end of the conference as I headed back to my table, my eye was drawn to an oatmeal raisin cookie, my favorite! I thought I had been so good for so long that one cookie would not hurt me. As I picked up the cookie, and anticipated its sweetness, I received something more than I expected: a word from the LORD. Literally, the moment that sweetness hit my taste buds, He whispered, "Taste and see that I am good." Just like it says in God's word. "Oh, taste and see that the Lord is good; Blessed is the man who trusts in Him!" (Psalm 34:8, NKJV)

What an invitation! God's desire was to prove His goodness? To me? What kind of love is that!? It was if God were saying, "I see you and I want you to see me. I want you to know Me!" I realized that something was required of me. I had to stop and taste and see. I could not simply pass by the table of the Lord's love and goodness. He had extended this blessing, but I had to accept it in order to come to know Him better and to receive all that He had for me. He called to me. He calls to us. He says, "Taste." God has given us all a hunger for Him. As babies, we are naturally hungry and know how to cry out until we are satisfied. As Christians He says, "Let the little children come to me, and do not hinder them, for the kingdom of God belongs to such as these" (Luke 18:16, NIV) and we should continue to cry out to Him to be nourished by His Word and His presence. Taste of God's goodness. See that He is Lord, so "that you may know what the hope of His calling is, what the riches of the glory of His inheritance in the saints." (Ephesians 1:18, NKJV) When the Lord says, "Taste and see," He is inviting us into an "experiential" relationship with HIM. This personal encounter with Him made me seek Him more than ever. I wanted to experience this "goodness," a kind of profound, divine goodness that I hadn't encountered before in the church.

Church had never been kind to me. I never felt accepted or had any sense of belonging. "Fellowship" was just a word tossed around in Christian circles and literature. I always felt like I was on the outside looking in. Despite my less than satisfying history, I knew I had to attend church in light of God's recent words to me. God had stirred up a fresh desire in me to seek Him out, but I was still grieving. This was going to require courage. Again, I had to choose.

I chose obedience, and God blesses obedience. He led me to a small Methodist church that was filled with the sweetest spirit. The people were kind and made me feel welcome. I never actually joined that church, but I did join the men's group, though with a somewhat reluctant heart. Being around men had always been difficult for me. Up to this point, I still had not experienced a relationship with a man that I could trust. Certainly I never trusted my alcoholic father, and the actions of most of the men I had known were worldly. I'm not saying that I lived a perfect life, but I learned that what most men did I didn't want to do. I saw that the things most men used to fill their void only left them feeling emptier. Meeting men of genuine Christian integrity had been a challenge, and many self-professed believers acted as if they were so "good" that their attitudes made me feel unworthy.

This was the backdrop to my new adventure with the Lord as I went to the men's group. I felt the fear and trepidation of a kid heading off to his first day of kindergarten, the difference now being that my Father came with me and I got to hold His hand the whole time. What I found was a truly beautiful core group of Godly but imperfect men who were willing to be transparent themselves, and to love me despite my imperfections. In my short time with them, they showed me that there are men who can be trusted. This was the prelude to genuine love and fellowship. How freeing this was for me. I do not think that they will ever know the full extent of the impact that their love has had on my life, and how their example taught me to love my brothers without judgment. May God receive glory for the great thing He did for me in this small group!

These men encouraged me into the next season of my life, even praying for me as I ventured out on my very first date. This was not just the first date since Diane's passing, but the first in my entire life. As a young man I could say that I honestly never really dated. There were a few awkward attempts, but I lacked self-confidence. So now, with the support of their fellowship, I began my four-year search for companionship. At one point the Lord specifically asked me, "Do you really like her?" about someone I had begun to see. "Yes," I replied because I really thought I knew myself.

What I learned is that when the Lord asks a question, He wants you to put a little more thought into the decisions that you are making. He has a plan for you, even if you cannot see it. Because I hastily said, "Yes, Lord," I felt the Holy Spirit back away. He did not stop blessing me, because He is a "Good, Good, Father," but He knew the beginning from the end. I did not pause to consider His question or my actions, and the relationship ended with regrets. Thankfully God's Word says in "And we know that all things work together for good to those who love God, to those who are the called according to His purpose." (Romans 8:28, NKJV) This experience completely changed my direction and attitude toward dating. I began to seek friendship rather than "relationships," knowing that God would eventually lead me to where He wanted me to be and who He wanted me to be with.

Despite the fact that I trusted God and knew I had to wait on Him, there was a constant longing that never left me. I had a deep desire for companionship. I've heard it said that the Lord puts desires in our hearts that only He can fill. "For it is God who works in you to will and to act in order to fulfill His good purpose." (Philippians 2:13, NIV) At this time, I'd been widowed for three years. I worked and had a home to care for, but though home was good, it was the house I had shared with my wife for twenty years and now shared with my daughter. I had never lived alone in my entire life. I was fifty-eight and finally ready to be on my own. I found it difficult to be surrounded by the former things and felt the desire for change.

I found a sweet little fixer upper in a wonderful little town called Santa Claus, Indiana. I devoted a lot of time and energy to transforming that house. Someone said to me during this season, "Isn't it good of God to give you this work to do at this time?" I was very conscious that the Lord had given me many good things to occupy my days. I was still working a 12-hour swing shift schedule. I had a hobby providing sound for a local band. I spent a lot of time at the YMCA. I travelled extensively from Iceland to Puerto Rico, from Hawaii to Florida, and cruised throughout the Caribbean with friends and family. I realized later that He provided a way for me to "Do business until I return." (Luke 19:13, AMP) He graciously kept me busy as I waited on Him.

The ironic thing is I'm not usually very good at waiting. As time passed, I slipped back into my old default position. It was natural for me to set out on my own to try to figure out what I should be doing. I began rushing ahead toward seemingly good goals. My work was fruitful but as I renewed my effort to "date," I experienced anxiety, emotional pain, and a fresh awareness of my lack rather than His abundance. I was *not* crying out to the Lord for my needs. Instead, I threw myself into the social abyss of over fifty singles. I fumbled and stumbled through this uncharted territory, which was more like interviewing strangers than actually enjoying another person's company. I discovered that my expectation of dating had very little to do with reality. I literally had no idea what I was doing. Whether good or bad, when you're married you are sheltered. I knew I was out of my depth and realized I truly needed to wait on the Lord for His best for me.

Time passed and there were many adventures … but still the void persisted. God's Word says, "And now these three remain: faith, hope and love. But the greatest of these is love." (1 Corinthians 13:13, NIV) Love continued to be the missing piece. The true desire of my heart had always been to love and be loved. Life, work, and many relationships had beaten me down because my hope for fulfillment and happiness was in those things. God was teaching me a new view and approach to love. He was also teaching me a new view of Him and was drawing me into a new relationship with Him. He was showing me that in fact, He was in control of every circumstance and was demonstrating once again that, "And we know that all things work together for good to those who love God, to those who are the called according to His purpose." (Romans 8:28, NKJV) The void or longing was the very thing that He used to compel me forward.

I decided I needed to connect with people in similar circumstances. I wasn't consoled by a world that hadn't experienced what I'd experienced. Research led me to a Christian support group for widows and widowers and there, I finally found real encouragement. One day, I received an interesting inquiry from a woman asking how the Lord had comforted me in my grief. She asked if I would be willing to share my story. I began to do a little investigation on who this woman was. I was surprised to find a woman whose grief had been transformed into a ministry. I happily responded the following day which "coincidentally" was my very first day of retirement. I had no idea that this simple conversation would be the key to a new life. I would come to understand that my suffering and awkward journey were purposeful, preparing me to be the hope of someone else's promise.

PART V

Honored Faith

CHAPTER 16

AN ARRANGED MARRIAGE

I have said so many times in this story, and felt so deeply throughout my widow's walk, that "I could not imagine...." That is the simple truth. I could never imagine what God had planned for my life. Could it really be full again? Was that an impossible dream? NO, not when it's a promise from God. It was my choice to believe, and I did. He saw my believing faith and honored His Word which says, "Therefore I tell you, whatever you ask for in prayer, believe that you have received it, and it will be yours" (Mark 11:24, NIV) and it also says, "If you believe, you will receive whatever you ask for in prayer." (Matthew 21:22, NIV) I didn't understand why I had to walk through the valleys that I'd walked through. But I always came back to Him who can do exceedingly and abundantly more than we could ever ask, imagine, or think. I could not have imagined all that God was doing to prepare another as I waited on and trusted in Him.

My first conversation with Bruce lasted about two hours and was filled with our strikingly similar stories, tears, and lighthearted optimism, but most importantly the sharing of our faith. I finally got an answer to my question about the other side of grief, the journey of the widower! I couldn't help but wonder, "Could this be him? NO, I have never even met him face to face! It doesn't work that way. Right?" From that day forward we spoke on the phone for 3 to 4 hours each day. How was this possible? After many, many conversations, I began to realize I was falling for this guy. I no longer glanced around wondering, "Is it this man? Is it that man over there?" It was such an effortless joy to speak to Bruce. I would often check my phone to see if he had texted me or if I had missed a call, because I just couldn't wait to talk to him.

Bruce introduced me to "Marco Polo," an app which allowed us to record and send video clips of our lives. It wasn't an actual conversation. It's like a visual walkie-talkie. I would send one clip and he would immediately respond. It was as if we were talking with a small delay. The amazing thing was that we could see each other for the first time, in our everyday surroundings. We filmed moments anywhere from the supermarket to the beach to the breakfast table. We "talked" and laughed until our sides ached and we couldn't breathe. Our families would inevitably walk in in the middle of our video conversations, so gradually we began to "meet" each other's loved ones. We happily showed each other our homes and our communities too. We came to know each other really well in a short time, though we had never actually met! How good was God to allow me to make a friend, to meet this man, without any threat or danger or obligation.

I was still making videos for my You Tube channel and video number 22 was "To Date or Not to Date." My friend Veronica cohosted this episode. We discussed the potential benefit of widening our small social circle beyond our families, friends, and church community. She signed us up for all kinds of extracurricular activities in order to expand our worlds. Veronica mentioned line dancing to which I exclaimed, "I have two left feet. I can't dance!" Ironically, this turned out to be the very catalyst that caused Bruce to act. I learned later that he decided in that moment, "If Suzie is going to widen her circle, I want to be in it!" He asked if he could come for a visit and offered to take Veronica and me out on a date. No pressure, all joy, guaranteed laughter. My immediate response was, "YES!" He bought a ticket the next day. I thought, "Wait! This is completely not like me. My goodness! What is going on? My Jesus, it's happening so quickly!"

The more we talked, the more we learned how many similarities our life stories shared. Obviously, we had both lost our loved ones. Our spouses both had the same rare aggressive kind of brain cancer. We both nursed them over the long term "til death do us part." We knew without words what the other had gone through. Both of our dads were alcoholics. We did not need to explain where we'd come from. Despite our childhood environments, we were both happily married for over thirty years. Neither of us knew anything about dating, having married our first loves. As young adults we both attended a CFC Church. We both had one boy (the eldest) and one girl (the youngest). It turned out that when Bruce was demolishing and rebuilding his house, I was doing the same thing to my house! We both thought of this as therapy. We both love DIY and projects in general. Bruce actually shares my love of decorating and design. We love the same food. We love our morning coffee. We have the same crazy sense of humor and love to laugh.

More important than all the similarities was the bond we felt, spirit to spirit. I had told Jesus, "I want my H2 and I to be like John the Baptist and Jesus in the womb, where their spirits recognized each other and leapt for joy while in their mothers' wombs." I have always been very specific when talking to the Lord. I didn't think that was too much to ask, because I always talk to Him about everything. I know He loves me and hears me and will do His perfect will regarding me, whether or not it's the answer I hoped for. I figure if I never ask God for anything specific, I may not recognize His hand or voice when the answer comes.

When the day finally came and I picked him up at the airport, I was so nervous that my mind, heart, and thoughts were all racing! I was as excited as a little girl waking up Christmas morning not knowing what I was going to find, but knowing what I hoped for. Then my eye caught a glimpse of him coming down the escalator and my heart melted. We promised not to kiss each other at the airport in front of strangers. Bruce totally broke his promise! Our souls knew full well in that moment, spirit to spirit, we had been brought together by God, in love, for His purposes. And so it began.

To the outsider, and even to members of my family, meeting Bruce may have seemed bold, maybe even foolhardy. However, he had been googled, vetted, and background-checked by my family and friends (all unbeknownst to him *or* me). Thankfully, he received an "all clear." Those who cared for me wanted to protect me. But after weeks of speaking face to face, for hours on end, I knew Bruce. I had complete trust and faith in him. I'd seen his heart, his tears, and heard his testimony. There was complete peace between us. I was confident and fearless.

We went to the Boat House restaurant in Rhode Island for our first face-to-face date and, since we both love salmon, we shared a yummy meal together. I thought wow, not too many guys would want to share! It was wonderful. I felt like I was floating. The following evening we had a wonderful birthday party for my mom, and my whole family got to meet (i.e., interview and inspect) him. Many times I jokingly told him that he was entering the "Everybody Loves Raymond" and "My

Big Fat Greek Wedding" family! My heart's desire was for them to see what I saw in him, a man of character, devotion, and love.

One test revealed his inner man just two days after Bruce arrived. I awoke in the middle of the night feeling very nauseous. I came downstairs and passed out twice! As I fell, I hit the side of my head near my eye and was on the floor for over an hour. For some strange reason I had my cell phone in my hand, and I had the wherewithal to call my son in his room upstairs. With all the strength I had, I whimpered, "Help me!" He called my mom, the nurse from her home next door at 2:00 a.m., and she realized they needed to rush me to the hospital. I had given Bruce my car to drive to his hotel just around the corner. He came right over and took me to the emergency room with my son.

On the drive to my house, Bruce had cried to the Lord, "WHY, Lord!? Why have You allowed this to happen just as I arrive?" He wondered why God would fill our hearts with love only to let them break again. But God answered immediately, "This is about character." I already knew who Bruce was, but Bruce's care, thoughtfulness, calm, and strength made him shine to others.

Apparently, your body doesn't like it when your potassium is low. This was the cause of my near-disaster. Low potassium causes your heart to beat irregularly, or "jiggle" as I like to say. "Jiggling" meant two days in the hospital. I now had a black eye, a swollen shoulder the size of a grapefruit, dirty stringy hair, bad breath, and no makeup. Even in my semiconscious state, I knew this wasn't how I wanted to present myself to this man who had just come 1,000 miles to meet me. For the next 48 hours, Bruce stayed by my side (brave man) and doted on me, bruises and all. My family was so grateful for the way he ministered to me, walking me around the halls at the hospital, bringing me meals, making me laugh, and so much more. I know firsthand that it's not always easy to blend families, but Bruce's behavior opened hearts and minds to who he truly was.

We thought we were going to have a weeklong "date," but God obviously had other plans. He used my short stay in the hospital to share our story, to declare how amazing He is and how He literally works in the lives of people. We were proof. The nurses were especially kind and attentive to us, and I remember one nurse coming in and saying what a cute couple we made, and how in love we looked! We laughed and said, "This is our second date!" We were good knowing that God was orchestrating all of this for His wonderful plan to touch people's lives and move in their hearts. At one point, I had to have a two-hour Nuclear Stress Test where they artificially make your heart go into high gear. The technician was actually searching for God and here I was. The Lord put me right in this guy's path. I told him about my awesome Lord, and he actually accepted my invitation to come to church.

During my procedure, Bruce went on a secret mission. The day I got out of the hospital, Bruce and I walked arm and arm to my SUV. I looked down and saw four brand-new tires. Wow! I'm very practical, and I loved this thoughtful, life-saving gift way better than flowers. My tires were almost bald, and God knew I needed new tires. In our weeks of video chatting, Bruce realized that I often drove my car when people needed help. He felt this gift would contribute to my ministry to others, and he was led to replace them as unto the Lord, not to gain approval from those close to me. I just leaned on him and cried.

From my hospital stay onward, our hearts were bound to each other. That doesn't mean everything else moved forward easily and seamlessly. There were so many things to work out. First of all, we hadn't even talked about getting married. He lived a thousand miles away from me. His daughter was getting married. My daughter was going to have a baby. He had two homes to care for and a lifetime of "stuff." I couldn't leave my homestead, family, and church. My mom had had a heart attack resulting in a serious car accident. And on it went. We both looked at the pros and cons of how this could even work, but God knows how to direct people and events in ways that only He can.

Over the course of the following months, we spent a week here and a week there together. Our time apart was heartache. We just didn't want to be separated any longer. We weren't babes in the woods. We had lived, struggled, and learned so much over the years and now we were ready to start a new life. On April 7, Bruce and I spoke for the first time. On April 23, Bruce heard a prophetic word declaring, "God is calling you to something new so don't be surprised if people don't understand it yet." Though we knew that the Lord brought us together and we were ready, our families "didn't understand it yet." It was important to us that we have their blessing but convincing them that we weren't crazy was going to be a challenge.

Fortunately, no challenge is too great for our God. It wasn't going to be easy, but we were certain that He would show our families that this was His plan. I took their concerns to heart. David Walker, my dear wise friend, counseled me "to move forward with the relationship hand in hand with God, but to guard my heart and not to become unrecoverable." He wanted, as did all those who loved me, to make sure I didn't go off the deep end emotionally. I was grateful for that. I'd never done anything like this in my entire life, but I had such clarity. I was not being rash. I was not a silly schoolgirl. I felt profoundly grounded walking in "the peace of God, which surpasses all understanding." (Philippians 4:7, ESV)

During my first trip to Indiana, Bruce planned a "Big Fat Greek

Wedding" party for all of his friends and family to meet me, as I had done for him. Although jokingly I said, "I don't want to take a visit to your hospital, so no fainting, no falling, no following in my footsteps." It was my turn in the hot seat. Bruce reassured me they would all love me like he did. He stood in front of everyone with a karaoke machine and sang a Keith Urban love song called "Memories of Us." Which basically said that he would be here for me, that he would be trustworthy, that no one would ever love me like him and though I have been stretched, it would be okay because he was here now. He sang about wanting to make forever memories with me.

The world around us disappeared and it was just Bruce and me. As I stared into his eyes, I saw into the depths of his heart and soul. I was completely in love. Right then and there, in secret and in plain sight, Bruce proposed to me through the words of that song. I looked around to see if anyone else saw what had just happened, but the rest of the world simply splashed in the pool and happily ate hotdogs, as Bruce committed his heart and his life to me. My heart overflowed! I just kept thanking the Lord, for I knew that my life had once again changed forever, but this time something other than grief consumed me. I was all in and so was Bruce. We were of one mind and one heart but would have to wait to see God's plan for our life together.

Flying away after that visit was wrenching. I knew I was leaving God's gift behind and planned another trip back soon after. On my second visit to Evansville, we decided to go to dinner. We held hands as we ordered appetizers. With one mind, we suddenly blurted out, "Are we doing this? Are we *really* doing this? Do you want to get *married*?" No ring, no plan, just completely of one accord. The rest came later. We just knew that we knew that we knew that God had arranged this marriage, so right then and there, we set a date for 9/12/17.

Needless to say that having known each other for only three months, we understood there would be resistance to the idea "in the natural." But this was already a supernatural union, and we were confident in God. There was no fear. We weren't blind to the realities, but we were 100 percent certain that this is what we had been called to. This is what we had been prepared for. As we looked at each other, we knew "this is the one."

I came back home and made a few more videos. I wanted to tell everyone what God was doing in my life, but felt I had to keep the secret a little while longer. Once we shared the news with our families, I decided to introduce Bruce as my fiancé in my next episode. Whenever we were in the same state from that time onward, we did a video together. In Episode #37, which I have named "Shock and Awww," you guessed it… Bruce got down on one knee and in front of the whole world, asked me to marry him.

Our engagement set things in motion. Bruce had just retired in April. Before he had even met me, the Lord told him that He would provide people to take care of his stuff. Bruce remembered wondering, "Hey, what's going to happen to me?" Now he understood. We had decided that we would live in Massachusetts, so he would need someone to care for his properties and possessions. The "people" were his sisters, Joyce and Rehnea, who had moved into his house to take care of what he would be leaving behind. He was "cleaning house," preparing for his own wedding, preparing for his daughter's wedding a couple of months after ours, arranging all of our honeymoon plans, and his list went on and on. I was searching for my dress, the venue for our wedding, preparing my home to accommodate my love. We were constantly in a frenzy of activity, but we both felt like teenagers. My constant thought was, "Lord, the plans You have for us are truly better than our own. Thank you for your grace towards us!"

The joyous day finally arrived: 09/12/17. We decided to get married at the Boat House, the place of our first date. My children were such an important part of this day for me. My very pregnant daughter orchestrated all the music while my son was our professional photographer. My best friend had discreetly obtained a license to marry us. It meant so much to me that this wonderful woman of God and steadfast friend would wed Bruce and me. Bruce's daughter came from Indiana to be her dad's "best man" and stood beside him as they waited for me to arrive. It was a gorgeous, warm day. Our friends and family gathered as the sun shimmered on the bay. I stood just outside the door with Randy as I waited for my cue. I looked up and smiled at the beautiful blue sky and silently asked, "Lord, do you see my heart? It's bursting with thankfulness to You. There are no words to describe how I feel at this moment. I know You ordained this day and are celebrating with us. I praise you, my Jesus."

I could not believe that this day had come. I was about to marry the man whom God had hand-chosen for me. I felt like I was floating. I heard the music and stepped forward with full confidence and love as I presented myself to my Bruce. He told me later that he was stunned as he stared at me, so thankful and in awe of the Lord. We wondered how He might use us as we began our journey as husband and wife. Our spirits just shouted together with joy, "Bring it, Lord!" and He wasted no time using us to minister to the brokenhearted in the very first days of our honeymoon. This delighted both of us. We knew that our union had a greater purpose than one we could have ever imagined, and we were excited to watch God work.

CHAPTER 17

A Greater Purpose

As I thought of the final chapter of this book, I wanted to remind you, the reader, of the beauty of God's Word. "For we are God's workmanship created in Christ Jesus for good works which God prepared beforehand, that we should walk in them." (Ephesians 2:10, ESV) We now know that God really did bring good out of our grief, and that He clearly knew all along the good works He had prepared in advance for Bruce and me to do. Whether ministering to one on a beach or thousands in a crowd, which has already happened, God has called us through very specific circumstances for a very specific purpose, and we are willing to answer His call.

It's extraordinary to look back at details that are revealed at a time when they are meaningless and may seem small, but later become stunningly significant. When Bruce checked out the date that Diane was diagnosed, I mentioned that that was something I hadn't done with Daryle's diagnosis. So I googled the dates around his diagnosis: 5, 6, 12, and 5, 7, 12; then I googled the dates around his death 5, 6, 13 and 5, 7, 13. I found them to be very interesting. The Strong's Hebrew concordance is an index which correlates Bible citations with word meanings. The dates I entered generated these definitions:

First two days = Congregation, Band, Writing, Book
Last two days = Secretary, Scribe, Testimony, Witness

David Walker had asked me if I wanted an Englishman, Irishman, Scotsman, or German. You ready? Genetic testing determined that Bruce was 25 percent of each of these ethnic groups!

Before we had even met, Bruce had heard a prophetic evangelist say, "God was moving amongst His people … arranging marriages for Kingdom ministry purposes." In particular, Bruce remembers that the prophecy mentioned that there were "books to be written." Little did he know at the time how intimately he would be involved in the writing of one of those books. We are amazed by how God has moved. We are married, in ministry to widows and widowers, writing a book. Neither one of us could have planned or produced this.

In our wildest dreams, we hadn't envisioned that God would so tangibly do for us what He promises to provide for those who grieve. "A joyous blessing instead of mourning." (Isaiah 61:3, NLT)

Remember when God called me His little flower? Imagine then, we are all planted on this earth by the Almighty in the garden of His choosing. No matter how small or delicate or how large and stately, we can present ourselves in such a way as to make the Master Gardener smile. Do not imagine that you are expendable, that your life has no meaning. Even as some flowers fall and fade away, it does not mean they didn't have purpose. God reveals that even in the falling there is purpose. "I tell you the truth, unless a kernel of wheat is planted in the soil and dies, it remains alone. But its death will produce many new kernels—a plentiful harvest of new lives." (John 12:24, NLT)

As I consider "purpose," I've come to the realization that our perception of purpose sometimes revolves around our own desires. We focus on what we hope to achieve while on planet earth. As believers, we can simply invite God to help us fulfill our dreams or, instead, we can invite Him to use us to fulfill His dreams. He's transformed my vision. I want my purpose to glorify Him in whatever way He chooses. We all experience trouble. Sometimes as we face trials and tribulations, we may feel we have little or no purpose, but God's Word states that He does have a plan for us and wants to complete it in our lives.

My own son shared with Bruce and me that he felt like his trials were refining him and that the Lord was preparing him as if his life were like a key. I thought that's an interesting way to put it. A key has to be forged with heat. It's then considered a blank that has to be put under pressure and precisely cut with valleys and peaks. Oftentimes, the blade goes in reverse to refine the pattern of the key. It's then buffed to remove excess burrs. Once completed it will be used by the maker to open the door it was specifically designed for *or* purposed for. The owner then keeps it until such a time as it has to be used. It is important because it has been uniquely crafted for one purpose. "This is the message from the one who is holy and true, the one who has the key of David. What He opens, no one can close; and what He closes, no one can open." (Revelation 3:7, NLT)

We feel God has shown us the door, and opened doors for us using our grief for a good purpose that He prepared in advance for us. Bruce and I will always have a heart for widows and widowers because once you walk through that particular valley, you never forget. We will continue to minister as the Lord leads, open to go wherever He sends us.

Please understand my heart when I say that this story is not a treasure map for finding a new spouse. No one can follow and duplicate the path of another. Look to God. He is the one who desires to work in your life and to reveal Himself personally to you. He is the one who has a unique plan for your life. Your purpose could be something completely different from what you've imagined. It could be marriage or it could very well be a new business, a new ministry, a move, or job change. Your purpose could be to stay home and raise your children. Whatever the Lord has planned for you, He will equip you for the task. Listen to His promise: "I am the Lord, and there is no other, besides me there is no God; I equip you, though you do not know me." (Isaiah 45:5, ESV)

Jesus says, "Here I am! I stand at the door and knock. If anyone hears my voice and opens the door, I will come in." (Revelation 3:20, NIV) It's His promise. He knows you. He wants to come in, so let Him in. You have nothing to lose and everything to gain. Answer His invitation and watch what He will begin to do in your life, take a step, believe, have faith because He says, "Now you will see whether or not what I say will come true for you." (Numbers 11:23, NIV)

Chronological Scripture Verses

"Now you will see whether or not what I say will come true for you." (Numbers 11:23, NIV)

"He defends the cause of the fatherless and the widow, and loves the foreigner residing among you, giving them food and clothing." (Deuteronomy 10:18, NIV)

"The secret things belong to the Lord our God, but the things revealed belong to us and our children forever." (Deuteronomy 29:29, ESV)

"And the Lord, He is the One who goes before you. He will be with you, He will not leave you nor forsake you; do not fear no be dismayed." (Deuteronomy 31:8, NKJV)

"And you shall be secure, because there is hope, yes, you shall dig about you, and you shall take your rest in safety." (Job 11:18, AKJV)

"When I consider Your heavens, the work of Your fingers, the moon and the stars, which You have set in place, what is mankind that You are mindful of them, human beings, that You care for them?" (Psalm 8:3–4, NIV)

"Surely You have granted him unending blessings and made him glad with the joy of Your presence." (Psalm 21:6, NIV)

"I will sing and make music to the Lord." (Psalm 27:6, NIV)

"Wait for the LORD; be strong and take heart and wait for the LORD." (Psalm 27:14, ESV)

"Oh, taste and see that the Lord is good; Blessed is the man who trusts in Him!" (Psalm 34:8, NKJV)

"The steps of good men are directed by the Lord. He delights in each step they take. If they fall, it isn't fatal, for the Lord holds them with His hand." (Psalm 37:23–24, TLB)

"All my longings lie open before You, Lord; my sighing is not hidden from You. My heart pounds, my strength fails me; Even the light has gone from my eyes. My friends and companions avoid me because of my wounds; my neighbors stay far away." (Psalm 38:9–11, NIV)

"The Lord sustains them on their sickbed and restores them from their bed of illness" (Psalm 41:3, NIV)

"God is our refuge and strength, always ready to help in times of trouble." (Psalm 46:1, NLT)

"[1]God is our refuge and strength,
an ever-present help in trouble.
[2]Therefore we will not fear, though the earth give way
and the mountains fall into the heart of the sea,
[3]though its waters roar and foam
and the mountains quake with their surging.
[4]There is a river whose streams make glad the city of God,
the holy place where the Most High dwells.
[5]God is within her, she will not fall;
God will help her at break of day.
[6]Nations are in uproar, kingdoms fall;
he lifts his voice, the earth melts.
[7]The Lord Almighty is with us;
the God of Jacob is our fortress.
[8]Come and see what the Lord has done,
the desolations he has brought on the earth.
[9]He makes wars cease
to the ends of the earth.
He breaks the bow and shatters the spear;
he burns the shields with fire.
[10]He says, "Be still, and know that I am God." (Psalm 46:1–10, NIV)

"Sing praises to God, Sing praises; Sing praises to our King, Sing praises!" (Psalm 47:6, NLT)

"Yes, my soul, find rest in God; my hope comes from him." (Psalm 62:5, NIV)

"They will still bear fruit in old age, they will stay fresh and green." (Psalm 92:14, NIV)

"Even in darkness light dawns for the upright, for those who are gracious and compassionate and righteous. Good will come to those who are generous and lend freely, who conduct their affairs with justice. Surely the righteous will never be shaken; they will be remembered forever. They will have no fear of bad news; their hearts are steadfast, trusting in the Lord." (Psalm 112:4–7, NIV)

"Because he bends down to listen, I will pray as long as I have breath!" (Psalm 116:2, NLT)

"I took my troubles to the LORD; I cried out to him, and he answered my prayer." (Psalm 120:1, NLT)

"Those who sow in tears will reap with songs of joy." (Psalm 126:5, NIV)

"Unless the Lord builds the house, its builders labor in vain." (Psalm 127:1, NIV)

"I will praise You, Lord, with all my heart; before the "gods" I will sing Your praise." (Psalm 138:1, NIV)

"When I called, you answered me; you made me bold and stout-hearted." (Psalm 138:3, NIV)

“The LORD will fulfill his purpose for me; your steadfast love, O LORD, endures forever. Do not forsake the work of your hands.” (Psalm 138:8, ESV)

“You saw me before I was born. Every day of my life was recorded in your book. Every moment was laid out before a single day had passed.” (Psalm 139:16, NLT)

“How precious are your thoughts about me, O God. They cannot be numbered!” (Psalm 139:17, NLT)

“Hope deferred makes the heart sick, but a dream fulfilled is a tree of life.” (Proverbs 13:12, NIV)

“He who finds a wife finds a good thing and obtains favor from the Lord.” (Proverbs 18:22, ESV)

“There is a time for everything, and a season for every activity under the heavens: a time to weep and a time to laugh, a time to mourn and a time to dance.” (Ecclesiastes 3:1, 4, NIV)

“For man does not know his time.” (Ecclesiastes 9:12, ESV)

“The grass withers and the flowers fall, but the Word of our God endures forever.” (Isaiah 40:8, NIV)

“Behold, I am doing a new thing; now it springs forth, do you not perceive it?” I will make a way in the wilderness and rivers in the desert.” (Isaiah 43:19, ESV)

"I am the Lord, and there is no other, besides me there is no God; I equip you, though you do not know me." (Isaiah 45:5, ESV)

"For your Maker is your husband, the Lord of hosts is his name." (Isaiah 54:5, ESV)

"The Spirit of the Lord God is upon me, because the Lord has anointed me to bring good news to the poor; He has sent me to bind up the brokenhearted, to proclaim liberty to the captives, and the opening of the prison to those who are bound;... to grant to those who mourn in Zion, to give them a beautiful headdress instead of ashes, the oil of gladness instead of mourning, the garment of praise instead of a faint spirit." (Isaiah 61:1, 3, ESV)

"A joyous blessing instead of mourning." (Isaiah 61:3, NLT)

"For he gives his sunlight to both the evil and the good, and he sends rain on the just and the unjust alike." (Matthew 5:45, NLT)

"Ask, it will be given to you; seek, and you will find; knock and it will be opened to you. For everyone who asks receives, and he who seeks finds, and to him who knocks, it will be opened." (Matthew 7:7–8, NIV)

"If you believe, you will receive whatever you ask for in prayer." (Matthew 21:22, NIV)

"Some fell on the rocky places, where it did not have much soil. It sprang up quickly, because the soil was shallow. But when the sun came up, the plants were scorched, and they withered because they had no root." (Mark 4:5–6, NIV)

"Therefore I tell you, whatever you ask for in prayer, believe that you have received it, and it will be yours." (Mark 11:24, NIV)

"Nothing is impossible for God!" (Luke 1:37, CEV)

"Why, even the hairs of your head are numbered." (Luke 12:7, ESV)

"Let the little children come to me, and do not hinder them, for the kingdom of God belongs to such as these." (Luke 18:16, NIV)

"Do business until I return." (Luke 19:13, AMP)

"The thief's purpose is to steal, kill and destroy. My purpose is to give them a rich and satisfying life." (John 10:10, NLT)

"I tell you the truth, unless a kernel of wheat is planted in the soil and dies, it remains alone. But its death will produce many new kernels—a plentiful harvest of new lives." (John 12:24, NLT)

"I have said these things to you, that in me you may have peace. In the world you will have tribulation. But take heart; I have overcome the world." (John 16:33, ESV)

"Abraham acted in faith when he stood in the presence of God, who gives life to the dead and calls into existence things that don't yet exist." (Romans 4:17, ISV)

"And we know that God causes all things to work together for good to those who love God, to those who are called according to His purpose." (Romans 8:28, NKJV)

"For I am persuaded that neither death nor life, nor angels nor principalities nor powers, nor things present nor things to come, nor height nor depth, nor any other created thing, shall be able to separate us from the love of God which is in Christ Jesus our Lord." (Romans 8:38–39, NKJV)

"Be glad for all God is planning for you. Be patient in trouble, and prayerful always." (Romans 12:12, TLB)

"Eye has not seen, nor ear heard, nor have entered into the heart of man the things which God has prepared for those who love Him." (1 Corinthians 2:9, NKJV)

"Take captive every thought to make it obedient to Christ." (2 Corinthians 10:5, NIV)

"And now these three remain: faith, hope and love. But the greatest of these is love." (1 Corinthians 13:13, NIV)

"That you may know what is the hope of His calling, what are the riches of the glory of His inheritance in the saints." (Ephesians 1:18, NKJV)

"For we are God's workmanship created in Christ Jesus for good works which God prepared beforehand, that we should walk in them." (Ephesians 2:10, ESV)

"Now all glory to God, who is able, through His mighty power at work within us, to accomplish infinitely more than we might ask or think." (Ephesians 3:20, NLT)

"The peace of God, which surpasses all understanding." (Philippians 4:7, ESV)

"For it is God who works in you to will and to act in order to fulfill His good purpose." (Philippians 2:13, NIV)

"Do not be anxious about anything, but in every situation, by prayer and petition, with thanksgiving, present your requests to God." (Philippians 4:6, NIV)

"Then you will experience God's peace, which exceeds anything we can understand. His peace will guard your hearts and minds as you live in Christ Jesus." (Philippians 4:7, NLT)

"I can do all this through Him who gives me strength." (Philippians 4:13, NIV)

"Whatever you do, work at it wholeheartedly as though you were doing it for the Lord and not merely for people." (Colossians 3:23, ISV)

"But the widow who lives for pleasure is dead even while she lives." (1 Timothy 5:6, NIV)

"Now faith is the substance of things hoped for, the evidence of things not yet seen." (Hebrews 11:1, NKJV)

"Therefore, since we are surrounded by such a great cloud of witnesses" (Hebrews 12:1, NIV)

"I will never leave you nor forsake you." (Hebrews 13:5, ESV)

"May He equip you with all you need for doing His will." (Hebrews 13:21, NLT)

"Consider it pure joy, my brothers and sisters, whenever you face trials of many kinds, because you know that the testing of your faith produces perseverance. Let perseverance finish its work so that you may be mature and complete, not lacking anything." (James 1:2–4, NIV)

"Come close to God, and I will come close to you." (James 4:8, NLT)

"This is the message from the one who is holy and true, the one who has the key of David. What He opens, no one can close; and what He closes, no one can open." (Revelation 3:7, NLT)

"Here I am! I stand at the door and knock. If anyone hears my voice and opens the door, I will come in." (Revelation 3:20, NIV)

Contact Information

Website: www.sueborrows.com
Email Suzie: sborrows7@hotmail.com
Email Bruce: blarue57@gmail.com
Email Editor: Diane Brown: dbwordsmith@gmail.com
YouTube: YouTube.com/widowswednesday
Facebook: Widows(ers)Walking With God
Website: www.hopeforwidows.org
Blog: www.rickyborrows.com
Walkers Website: www.biblemissionsinc.com
Pimentel Website: www.householdoffaith.mobi